What Really Happened to Jesus

What Really Happened to Jesus

A historical approach to the resurrection

Gerd Lüdemann

in collaboration with Alf Özen

Translated by John Bowden

 Westminster John Knox Press
Louisville, Kentucky

Translated by John Bowden from *Was mit Jesus wirklich geschah; Die Auferstehung historisch betrachtet*, published 1995 by Radius-Verlag, Stuttgart

© Radius-Verlag GmbH Stuttgart 1995

Translation © John Bowden 1995

Cover design by Kim Wohlenhaus

Cover illustration: The Dead Christ, with Angels, Edouard Manet (French 1832–1883), oil on canvas; from the H.O. Havemeyer Collection (29.100.51). Bequest of Mrs H.O. Havemeyer, 1929. Used by permission of The Metropolitan Museum of Art.

First American edition 1995

Published by Westminster John Knox Press, Louisville, Kentucky

Library of Congress Cataloging-in-Publication Data

Lüdemann, Gerd.
   [Was mit Jesus wirklich geschah. English]
   What really happened to Jesus : a historical approach to the Resurrection / Gerd Lüdemann in collaboration with Alf Özen. — 1st ed.
      p.   ca.
   Translated by John Bowden.
   Includes bibliographical references.
   ISBN 0–664–25647–3
   1. Jesus Christ—Resurrection   I. Özen, Alf. II. Title.
BT481.L8613   1996
232'.5—dc20   95–35036

Printed in Great Britain

Preface

My book *The Resurrection of Jesus. History, Experience, Theology*, appeared in German in spring 1994 and in English later that year. The arguments developed in it met with a lively response in Germany. They were passionately rejected in circles which regarded questioning of the bodily resurrection of Jesus as a betrayal of the gospel, and legal proceedings against the author were called for. For others, who regarded themselves as modern Christians, what the book said about the corruption of the body of Jesus went too far. They criticized it for over-rating historical research and under-rating theology. Still, despite all the objections and opposition, since then the book has begun something: it has started a ferment which is serving to clarify what we are to understand by resurrection.

However, some people have complained that the book is too academic, too detailed and difficult for lay people to understand. This, they argue, is making the study of the resurrection which is beginning in some churches difficult or even preventing it. I concede that the sometimes minutious search for truth must often concern itself with what are seen as minor points of detail. But it is precisely these 'snippings' which when all taken together often result in a correct understanding of the overall picture. That is how academic research must proceed if it is to arrive at well-founded results. So my larger book on the resurrection could not be, nor was it meant to be, easy to read.

The more popular version offered here is meant to meet the often-expressed desire for the results of academic research to be made more easily accessible to non-specialists. So it is deliberately aimed at an interested lay audience. To achieve this, some of the text of the larger book has had to be considerably reworked. Alf Özen has undertaken this in collaboration with me.

Many passages not absolutely necessary for an overall understanding have been deleted, including most of the notes. Those who are looking for evidence or bibliographical references for the arguments put forward in the book should refer to the larger edition. At the same time some explanations have been added to the book on matters which can be taken for granted in writing for specialists but cannot be assumed to be known by non-theologians. I hope that the argument will now be easier to follow. The English translation on which the book is based is that of the Revised Standard Version.

If this edition helps to carry the discussion of the resurrection of Jesus into the public sphere, into churches and schools, and thus pave the way for a process of clarification over this question which is so central to Christian faith, its main purpose will have been achieved.

Gerd Lüdemann

Contents

I

Introduction

The resurrection of Jesus is the central point of the Christian religion. Its significance in the church and in theology is immense. Every day pastors comfort mourners with the message of the resurrection of the dead; the church derives its right to exist from the authority bestowed on it by the risen Christ; and the risen Christ still serves academic theology as a guarantee for theological epistemology, as these quotations from three distinguished theologians indicate:

> The question of the resurrection of Jesus Christ poses a key question, perhaps even *the* key question, of Christian faith. Even though the average Christian is hardly aware of the fact, almost all other questions of faith and theology are decided by this question.[1]

> Christianity stands or falls with the reality of the raising of Jesus from the dead by God.[2]

> Christianity, in so far as it is the confession of Jesus of Nazareth as the living and powerfully effective Christ, begins at Easter. Without Easter there is no gospel . . . no faith, no proclamation, no church, no worship, no mission.[3]

Evidently everything quite simply depends on the event of the resurrection of Jesus. But what are we really to understand by 'resurrection of Jesus'? If we look more closely at the event, on all sides we get only woolly and often evasive answers.

'God raised Jesus from the dead.' Fine, but what actually happened? How did people come to this conclusion? The theologian Willi Marxsen claims:

> For my faith in Jesus, it is completely unimportant how Peter arrived at his faith in Jesus after Good Friday. It is equally unimportant how the person found faith who then communicated

his faith to me, so that I, in my turn, could believe . . . The decisive thing is that the faith is always *the same* . . . Our faith is only the Christian faith if it is joined with the faith of the first witnesses and with the faith of Peter.[4]

These statements lead us to ask how someone who talks about faith like this knows anything about the faith in the first century which he or she wants to share. One suspects that the statements about Jesus' resurrection which appear in the Bible, the mere wording, are enough for most Christians to establish the fact of the resurrection. They can thus treat this as an event established in the best possible way.

This observation is all the more suspicious given that the 'resurrection' of Jesus has largely become an indispensable requisite of theology and at the same time an empty formula. For at the same time there is anxiety in wide Christian circles that academic research could produce results which could put the traditional content of faith in question. If the foundations of faith are shaken, either by a timid enquiry or as a convinced assertion, a cry of indignation can be heard from the supposed guardians of the faith: 'Just don't shake it', seems to be the slogan. 'Perhaps we might prove to have built on sand. But if we have, please, we don't want to know.'

Many Christians today have lapsed into a degree of split consciousness. The hallowed precincts of church and theological tradition often stand directly opposed to the human sense of truth. If no bridge can be built here, then all is up with the credibility of theology and the church, and for all their apparent splendour, both are heading for *rigor mortis*. But how does the practical approach look today? Too many people certainly share the following experience of Karl Jaspers:

For me, one of the pains of a life of concern for the truth is that discussion with theologians stops at decisive points: they fall silent, utter an incomprehensible sentence, talk about something else, make some unconditional assertion, speak in a kind and friendly way without having noticed what one has just said – and in the end probably have no real interest in it. For on the one hand they feel confident, terrifyingly confident, in their truth, and on the other they don't seem to think it worth while bothering with us people who seem so stubborn. But to talk together calls for attention and a real answer; it prohibits silence or the avoidance of questions; above all it requires any statement of faith, which after all is made in human language, which is directed at objects and is a disclosure in the world, to be put in question and examined again, not only externally but also internally.[5]

Now if someone raises a finger and has the audacity to put a specific question, 'Resurrection? How am I to imagine that? In our modern age I can no longer believe that dead bodies are raised', then the answer, 'That is the case – you must simply believe it firmly', at best brings temporary reassurance. The question keeps arising, 'What really happened?'

If this question were easy to answer, then there would not be constant cause for discussion. The problem has been the same for centuries. The witnesses which we have within the Bible do not describe the resurrection. They report what was experienced, and just as anything experienced is interpreted and reported differently by those who experience it, so too these testimonies are full of inconsistencies and sometimes contradictions.

However, one thing is certain. The resurrection of Jesus had an incomparable effect. Historically it was of decisive significance for the rise and ongoing development of the Christian tradition.

Each age has its own possibilities for using science and research to enquire into and interpret the distant past. Today the possibilities of historical research are so developed that it is worth approaching old problems and questions afresh and seeking contemporary answers.

The need for renewed work on the resurrection of Jesus arises above all because this event has been handed down by historicizing reports. Therefore 'the reliability and credibility of this side of the act of revelation which is turned towards history must be examined'.[6] The question of the foundation and justification of this testimony remains the decisive one. For without this foundation, any theology of the resurrection, even New Testament theology, is groundless speculation.

Now the purpose of a historical work on the resurrection of Jesus is not new, and the arguments against such an investigation are well known. I shall take up the most important ones, which in part overlap:

1. We have no eye-witness accounts of the resurrection of Jesus

At any rate we have the statements of Paul in his letters and the accounts in Acts. At the same time, these throw light on the other testimonies to the resurrection, since Paul puts his own 'encounter' with the risen Christ on the same level as that with the other witnesses (I Cor.15.8). Moreover, is not the question of the nature of the resurrection a necessary one as long as Christian theology claims to be a scientific discipline and is aware of its indebtedness to the Enlightenment? Of course whether any results can be achieved (and if so, what results) is another matter. For the moment I am concerned merely to emphasize the duty to ask about the 'manner' of the resurrection.

2. The traditions about the resurrection cannot be disentangled and the historical sources are inadequate

The church historian Hans von Campenhausen has rightly objected to this argument. A reference to the tangle in the sources only helps what thinks of itself as especially radical faith 'to avoid its own tribulations by means of history and historical reason'.[7] In other words, to say that what really happened at Easter is inexplicable seems formally to become a necessary ingredient of theology. But the argument that a question cannot be answered does not settle that question. This assertion does not relieve historical research of its obligation to investigate; on the contrary, it makes it all the more necessary. For changed times with changed or refined methods of research might very well find an answer. Therefore what is needed is a persistent desire to know, which is not satisfied with what has been achieved.

3. The resurrection of Jesus is a miracle which completely evades our grasp – what can historical work achieve here?

Indeed the miraculous or revelatory character of Jesus cannot be the object of scientific *historical* work; it can only be the object of philosophical and theological reflection. But as long as theology is virtually 'paired' with historical thought, as it is on the one hand because of the character of its textual sources and what they say and on the other because of our modern awareness of truth, it must be interested in the manner of the resurrection of Jesus. An answer to the question how the resurrection of Jesus came to be asserted is unavoidable for an understanding of how the resurrection was proclaimed at that time and how this proclamation can be continued or reformulated today.

4. It is impossible to talk meaningfully about the resurrection of Jesus outside the experience of faith and Christian testimony. 'To put the question of the resurrection exclusively in historical terms is to alienate the texts of the Easter narratives.'[8]

This argument is out of this world. Everything ends up in 'I believe in order to understand', a statement which cannot be left unquestioned in the context of modern scholarship. As long as absurdity is not to be made the criterion of the truth of theological statements, academic theologians (*and* preachers in church) must be concerned for their remarks to be comprehensible. In other words, the science of theology has the task of ascertaining and interpreting Christian testimonies of faith from history and today. Theology and preaching do not primarily share in this work.

It is not the case that scientific research has to capitulate to matters of faith, as is often asserted. For believing, too, is first evoked by something. Thus there is always some event behind it. So the investigation of testimonies of faith also serves to bring us one step nearer to this evocation of faith, which is really inexpressible. However, how near we can come to it must be a matter for discussion.

5. Event and interpretation are always interlocked, so that it is impossible to have access to the event of the resurrection without the interpretation.

The interlocking of event and interpretation applies to all texts with which the historian deals and thus is in no way a peculiarity of religious or Christian source texts. For of course every author tries to describe something particular (e.g. an event) with his or her own individual capacities. It is evident that this can always be only his or her own wholly personal, subjective interpretation, which is more or less close to what is described. This normal fact is an occasion for perceiving and respecting every given source as an expression of human life. An event may by no means be identified with its interpretation in texts.

However, that cannot and may not keep us from investigating the New Testament texts in search of material which can be utilized for history, taking their character into account. Experience shows us that what a text is saying is disclosed anew if we approach it with all the scientific means at our disposal.

So in what follows I shall make a purely historical investigation into the historical context of the testimonies to the resurrection. In short, I shall ask how the resurrection of Jesus came about. My aim is to present a hypothesis about the resurrection which presents the fewest obstacles and resolves the most difficulties.

It is almost superfluous to say that the accounts which follow move within the realm of the probable and that the limits to this investigation are thus set *a priori*. Possible objections like 'purely hypothetical' rest on a misunderstanding of historical work. Like any form of interpretation, historical reconstruction cannot proceed without hypotheses and assessments of probability. Indeed it is the real task of historical investigation to work out the most appropriate hypotheses and carefully weigh probabilities in the process. The value of a reconstruction is decided by whether it is based on the best hypotheses, i.e. those which answer the most (and most important) open questions or solve existing problems, and provoke the least (or only weak) counter-arguments. So the duty of a historian is comparable to the task of a court of law: to examine the witnesses and reconstruct the probable course of events.

An investigation in this form with its aims and possible answers is important for the theological question as long as theology maintains the relationship to history and critical research which it has had since the Enlightenment.

2

The Theme

The texts

To reconstruct the events following Jesus' death it is necessary to survey all the information at our disposal which may allow inferences about what happened at the time. The relevant texts appear in the New Testament in the four Gospels and also in Acts and the Pauline literature, and in some works which are not part of the New Testament, the so-called 'Apocrypha'. However, before the investigation proper, a word needs to be said about how these texts are to be assessed generally.

The letters of Paul are the earliest texts of the New Testament and come from the years (40) 50–60. Only later did the Gospel of Mark appear (c.70) and then the Gospel of Luke (c.80), the Gospel of Matthew (c.85), Acts (c.90) and finally the Gospel of John (c.100). However, caution is needed: the probable chronological order in which the texts were written does not in itself determine the value of their content. The age of a text is not necessarily evidence of its 'accuracy'. One cannot simply say that because a text is old, what it says is trustworthy, and because another is later, what it says is less trustworthy. For after circulating for a long time in oral or even written form, old traditions could have been incorporated into a literary work composed at a late stage, which would then contain the earliest elements of tradition despite its late date. This must be noted in the analysis.

It is generally recognized that none of the Gospels was written by companions or close associates of Jesus. People whom for more or less plausible reasons we call Matthew, Mark, Luke and John shaped the text in the form in which we now have it.

Moreover, the occurrence of the same passages in several Gospels in wording which is very similar does not mean that such texts intrinsically have a greater truth content. It is particularly important to note this point in comparing the Gospels of Matthew, Mark and Luke. For scholars generally recognize that the authors of the Gospels of Matthew and Luke use the Gospel of Mark in their works. Moreover they also had access to a collection containing sayings of Jesus which scholars generally refer to as Q (for German *Quelle*, 'source'). This explains why in so many passages these three Gospels sound the same. In addition, however, Matthew and Luke offer narratives which Mark did not yet know. Furthermore, all the Gospels contain reports which have no parallels in the other Gospels. The explanation of this is often that here there are 'local traditions' which an author knew because of the place where he lived (because the stories were told there), and others did not, because they lived in areas where these stories were unknown. The situation is more complicated for the Gospel of John, because it is often unclear which sources John used.

So the 'evangelists' could refer back to a wealth of material which came into being at different times and in different places. Thus in the Gospels, alongside traditions of a later date, traditions are used whose origin dates back to the days of the 'historical Jesus'. In general they are reactions to concrete events. If a particular remark of Jesus made an impression on his hearers, it was handed down. The context in which it was made might be lost. There may have been sayings which were important to one particular person who handed them on. Another perhaps noted other sayings of Jesus or none at all. Thus fragments were handed down by word of mouth, many of them in small collections, loosely associated, before they were finally written down. In the interim a little story was often constructed around a saying of Jesus. That helped such a saying to be remembered and retold much better. The evangelists now brought many of these fragments together into large complexes, the Gospels. In so doing they were guided by the desire to relate the life, death and resurrection of Jesus. All the evangelists worked out a narrative framework for this into which they fitted the traditions at their disposal. In this way our Gospels came into being, from reminiscences of Jesus which often were out of context.

It is certain that Jesus was crucified around the year 30. But the earliest Gospel, Mark, in its final form comes from around the year 70. So about forty years had passed in the meantime. If we reflect how many details could have been lost in the course of forty years, how stories could have changed in such a period, be elaborated, and how in addition legends could form, we can understand that *a priori* not every word of the Gospels may be understood as the description of an actual event. A distinction must be made between sentences or words of the evangelists themselves (e.g. transitions between individual stories) and what they had at their disposal, the traditions. These traditions in turn need independent investigation. They are not all of equal age, nor do all contain historical events. Thus for example miracle stories have been added to emphasize the uniqueness of Jesus. Now again that does not mean that all the miracle stories are complete inventions. So it is also the task of scientific research to make and justify these and similiar distinctions.

Now what makes the reconstruction of events even more difficult is the fact that the evangelists were not neutral observers. They were all Christians, and they interpreted all the reports about the Jew Jesus as Christians. They believed in Jesus as their risen Lord. Jesus is always depicted in the Gospels as the risen Lord, even when they are really about the itinerant preacher Jesus travelling through the land, a man of whom the disciples did not yet have the remotest idea that he would be crucified and subsequently even raised from the dead.

So the Gospels interpret past events each from its own later perspective. However, this is not objective historiography. Everything that they say must therefore at first be treated with scepticism. Here is the greatest difficulty which we face if what is reported in the Gospels is to be reconstructed and evaluated. Only a criticial investigation of what the texts say, which attempts to penetrate to the historical nucleus through all the legends and elaborations surrounding it, can allow us to conjecture what really happened. Historical facts with this degree of probability are indispensable for rooting our Christian faith in history.

Mode of procedure

The testimony of Paul in I Corinthians 15.1–11 is the earliest text in the New Testament to make concrete mention of the death, resurrection and appearances of the risen Christ. Here Paul uses traditions which he knows from an earlier period. As I Corinthians is usually dated around 50, we may note, first, that the traditions which he mentions must be even older. Just how old remains to be seen.

This early text will be the guideline for our investigations. An attempt will be made to establish the age of the traditions, to illuminate the situation in which they came into being, and to discover what historical events lie behind them.

Paul wrote I Corinthians for a quite definite purpose. He was not concerned to give a precise account of *how* Jesus died and what his resurrection appearances were like. Evidently the only important thing for Paul in this situation was *that* they had taken place (Jesus died around 30; the events which Paul mentions here thus lay around twenty years in the past).

Accordingly an investigation of this text will produce only very incomplete results. So following that, every aspect mentioned in it needs to be discussed separately, and at length, using all the other available sources.

The point of entry:
I Corinthians 15.1–11

Paul founded the community in Corinth in around 41,[9] when he was on his so-called Second Missionary Journey. He knew many members of the community personally from that time. So in I Corinthians he is writing to people whom he knows well.

One does not write to people with whom one can presuppose common ground in the same way as one does to strangers. Not every topic needed to be elaborated to the smallest detail; it was enough to mention key words which were known to those to whom Paul was writing. That also explains the brief mentions of the death and resurrection of Jesus: no further detailed information was necessary.

1. Now I would remind you, brethren, in what terms I preached to you the gospel, which you received, in which you stand,
2. by which you are saved, if you hold fast – unless you believed in vain.
3. For I delivered to you as of first importance what I also received, that Christ died for our sins in accordance with the scriptures,
4. that he was buried, that he was raised on the third day in accordance with the scriptures,
5. and that he appeared to Cephas, then to the twelve.

6. Then he appeared to more than five hundred brethren at one time, most of whom are still alive, though some have fallen asleep.

7. Then he appeared to James, then to all the apostles.

8. Last of all, as to one untimely born, he appeared also to me.

9. For I am the least of the apostles, unfit to be called an apostle, because I persecuted the church of God.

10. But by the grace of God I am what I am, and his grace towards me was not in vain. On the contrary, I worked harder than any of them, though it was not I, but the grace of God which is with me.

11. Whether then it was I or they, so we preach and so you believed.

In vv.3b–8 Paul mentions the death, resurrection and appearances of Christ. Here he is remembering something already known to the Corinthians, namely a kind of confession of faith of the early Christians which he had handed on at the foundation of the community. Two things in particular suggest that this extends only from v.3b to the end of v.5 ('then to the twelve'): (a) after 'then to the twelve' another sentence construction begins; (b) as the words 'most of whom are still alive, though some have fallen asleep' (v.6b) are certainly not part of the tradition which Paul handed on in the visit when he founded the church, it might seem probable that here Paul is no longer recalling what the Corinthians already know. Rather, he is relating something new, using different traditions. The purpose of this is probably on the one hand to provide 'historical' support for the resurrection of Jesus: more than 500 witnesses all at once (v.6a) cannot be wrong, and if anyone was still sceptical about what they had heard they could ask them directly, since most of them were still alive (v.6b). Secondly, Paul was evidently concerned to continue down to himself the tradition which he brought to the Corinthians on the visit on which the community was founded, and which certainly already included the appearance of Jesus to Cephas. That being so, it was necessary to add appearances of the same kind as those which preceded his own chronologically, so that it would become clear that according to v.8 Paul had received the same 'vision' as all the other people cited in this list. The appearances to Cephas and James (vv.5,7) which originally probably had the role of endorsing the first visit and thus legitimizing Cephas and James, were now used by Paul to confirm the fact of the resurrection of Christ as such.

We now know that vv.3b–8, which interest us, consist of three parts:

1. What Paul preached when he founded the community (vv.3b–5);
2. Further resurrection appearances (vv.6,7);
3. The last resurrection appearance to Paul himself (v.8).

The various statements in I Corinthians 15.3b–5

It rapidly becomes clear that the tradition in vv.3-5, handed down on the visit on which Paul founded the community, is unequal in character: here the fourfold 'that', which perhaps goes back to Paul himself, also indicates a sequence of different formulae. Thus the statements about the resurrection of Jesus and Jesus' death 'for our sins' originally did not stand side by side, as comparative texts indicate,[10] but were put together only at a later stage (cf. the similar combination of statements about the death and resurrection in Rom.4.25; 14.9; II Cor.5.15; I Thess.4.14). However, it is not yet clear *when* this connection was made. It need not come from Paul, but it may already be old and may have been used by Paul here in an already finished form.

In addition we can also see that vv.3b–5 offer a twofold proof, (a) from the scriptures (we know them as the 'Old Testament') and (b) from confirmation by facts. Accordingly, vv.3b–5 consist of two parts and are to be read as follows:

(a) Christ died for our sins according to the scriptures and he was buried;

(b) he was raised on the third day according to the scriptures and appeared to Cephas, then to the twelve.

There are different views about the origin of the piece of tradition in I Cor.15.3b–5. One trend of scholarship derives it from the Greek-speaking communities around Antioch and Damascus (with whom Paul had particularly close contact); another derives it from the Aramaic-speaking earliest community in Jerusalem, in which case we must presuppose a translation into Greek. On the whole the alternative 'Jerusalem or Antioch?' here seems to be exaggerated. 'For even if the tradition came to Paul via the church in Antioch, this would only have handed on what it had received – from

Jerusalem.'[11] Moreover, an argument in terms of content suggests Jerusalem as the origin of the tradition: the closing remark in I Cor.15.11 that Paul's preaching corresponds with that of the others mentioned, i.e. the original apostles – and initially these were in Jerusalem.

The relationship between the appearances to Peter and to James

We now come to the question of the first appearance of Jesus to Cephas/Peter (v.5) and its relationship to the appearance of the Risen Christ (christophany) to James (v.7).

The statement in v.5, 'he appeared to Cephas, then[12] to the twelve', can be detached as an independent unit from the tradition handed down by Paul on the visit in which he founded the Corinthian community as an independent unit. This is suggested, first by the parallel to Luke 24.34 ('The Lord is truly risen and has appeared to Simon') and Mark 16.7 ('Say to his disciples and Peter'), and secondly, by the parallel formula in v.7 which follows.

The christophany to James (and all the apostles) in I Cor.15.7 contains two statements: first, that James received an appearance, and secondly, that James has a special position in the apostolic circle.

It is striking that vv.5 and 7 have the same construction and that the same words are used – apart from Cephas/James and the twelve/all the apostles: 'he appeared to Cephas, then to the twelve'; 'he appeared to James, then to all the apostles'. This parallelism could be explained in two ways: (a) here Paul was modelling his language in v.7 on v.5, in which he was using a tradition about an appearance to James and all the apostles; (b) Paul was reproducing an independent tradition in both cases. In the latter case either the one formula had already been modelled earlier on the basis of the others, or both formulae have a common origin. At all events, it is clear that there is an earlier tradition in both v.5 and v.7.

The traditions handed down in I Cor.15.5,7 contain the brief report that the risen Christ had appeared to a particular group of Christians. The possible function of such a 'formula' becomes clear from a look at Paul's writings. Paul refers to his vision of the risen Christ at many points in his battle against his opponents (I Cor.9.1, 'Have I not seen Jesus our Lord?'; cf. Gal.1.15f., 'that he [= God] revealed his son in me that I should proclaim him through the gospel among the Gentiles'; Phil.3.8, 'the surpassing worth of knowing Jesus Christ, my Lord') to legitimate his authority. The traditions in I Cor.15.57 probably have a similar function and are therefore best termed 'legitimation formulae'.

The competition between the two formulae in vv.5 and 7 is understandable if we connect them with the development of the earliest community in Jerusalem in the first two decades of its existence. According to them, the first appearance was to Peter. For the formula legitimating Peter and the twelve is earlier than that of I Cor.15.7. It comes from the period when the group of twelve was still in existence (the group did not continue long after Jesus' death) and was already associated at the time with the early confession of faith in vv.3b, 4, i.e. the connection was not first made by Paul.

In the subsequent period, James, the brother of Jesus, became increasingly influential in the earliest community, until he finally became its sole leader.

So the text I Cor.15.7 comes from a later period, when followers of James (or James himself) claimed that James was the first witness. For this purpose they assimilated the report of the appearance of Jesus to James to I Cor.15.5. This does not put in question the fact of an appearance of the risen Jesus to James; moreover he certainly 'saw' Jesus at an early period, when Peter was still leader of the community. But only at a later date was James claimed as first witness.

Interim result

All the pieces of tradition investigated here (death, burial, resurrection, appearances) came into being at a very early date. We can assume that all the events reported in them are to be dated to the first couple of years after the crucifixion of Jesus. At all events this theory is probable for I Cor.15.3b–5. However, I Cor.15.6a,7 also provides compelling reasons for putting the conversion of Paul at the chronological end of the appearances listed, and this is to be thought of as being soon after the death of Jesus, which is generally put around the year 30.

A fairly certain date can similarly be worked out for the conversion of Paul as well. The Acts of the Apostles credibly reports a stay of Paul in Corinth when Gallio was there as governor of Achaia (Acts 18). Now this Gallio was in office in 51/52.[13] If we calculate back from this date the intervals which Paul mentions in Gal.1.18 ('three years') and 2.1 ('fourteen years'), and add two years for travelling, the date of his conversion comes out at around 33.

So we may state that *the appearances mentioned in I Cor.15.3–8 took place in the time between 30 and 33 CE (the fact of the appearances) because the appearance to Paul is the last in this list and is not to be dated later than 33 CE. The final form of its tradition (what the appearances were like) had not yet been fixed.*

Now I have already remarked that in his preaching when the community was founded Paul merely handed on the 'confession of faith' mentioned above and the appearance to Cephas and the twelve, but did not mention any further appearances of Christ (e.g. like that to more than five hundred brothers). Then followed the reason why the apostle listed these appearances in I Corinthians: to provide historical guarantees of the resurrection of Jesus and to guarantee his own apostolic authority. It is obvious that here he was proceeding with great care in his own interest. From this it follows for the text, first, that Paul cited all the appearances known to him; and secondly, that the information was highly reliable and complete.

At this point the question arises why Paul did not report the other appearances in his preaching at the founding of the community. The answer is that they were not (yet) the basis of salvation, like the 'creed' of the death and resurrection of Jesus, whereas the appearance(s) to Cephas and the twelve in the earliest period had a special significance in founding the church and therefore were part of the gospel. We cannot conclude from this that the other appearances took place historically only after the foundation of the Corinthian community. Such an assumption already comes to grief on the fact that e.g. the appearance to more than 500 brethren is told for the simple reason that it really happened. Paul may perhaps not yet have known these traditions when he founded the community in Corinth.

It is still hard to say what the relationship was between the event itself and the development of the description of it. Because of the extraordinary nature of the event in question we may suppose that it was also reported immediately after the appearance of Jesus. How could it be conceivable that an event took place and was only related, shall we say, ten years later?

That indicates the following traditions in I Cor.15.1-11 which were handed down shortly after Jesus' death:

1. Jesus died (I Cor.15.3b);
2. Jesus was buried (I Cor.15.4a);
3. Jesus was raised on the third day (I Cor.15.4b);
4. Jesus appeared to particular witnesses (I Cor.15.5–8);
   (a) He appeared to Cephas/Peter (I Cor.15.5a);
   (b) He appeared to the twelve (I Cor.15.5b);
   (c) He appeared to more than 500 brothers (I Cor.15.5);
   (d) He appeared to James (I Cor.15.7a);
   (e) He appeared to all the apostles (I Cor.15.7b);
   (f) He appeared to Paul (I Cor.15.8).

Starting from this list and on the basis of all available texts I shall now investigate what historical events we may assume to be behind these traditions – of the burial, resurrection and resurrection appearances of Jesus.

3

The Events after Jesus' Death

The death of Jesus

The fact of the death of Jesus as a consequence of crucifixion is indisputable, despite hypotheses of a pseudo-death or a deception which are sometimes put forward. It need not be discussed further here.

The burial of Jesus

The earliest account of the burial of Jesus that we have (I Cor.15.3f.) leaves its details open, just as the note about his death given there does not mention the manner of dying (crucifixion). Nevertheless an attempt must be made to trace the burial of Jesus.

The burial itself is reported in early Christian writings in two forms:

(a) Joseph of Arimathea buried Jesus (Mark 15.42–47 and parallels in the Gospels of Luke, Matthew and John);

(b) Jews buried Jesus (John 19.31–37).

But what really happened? Do the texts allow us to make any inferences about this event?

The report in Mark 15.42–47
and its parallel passages

The best-known German-speaking New Testament scholar of this century, Rudolf Bultmann, regards the text of Mark 15.42–47 as a historical account which does not sound like a legend.[14] However, even he cannot establish how old the tradition contained here is. In order to examine his judgment the passage must be looked at in its overall context, Mark's account of the passion:

> 42. And when evening had come, since it was the day of Preparation, that is, the day before the sabbath,
>
> 43. Joseph of Arimathea, a respected member of the council, who was also himself looking for the kingdom of God, took courage and went to Pilate, and asked for the body of Jesus.
>
> 44. And Pilate wondered if he were already dead; and summoning the centurion, he asked him whether he was already dead.
>
> 45. And when he learned from the centurion that he was dead, he granted the body to Joseph.
>
> 46. And he bought a linen shroud, and taking him down, wrapped him in the linen shroud, and laid him in a tomb which had been hewn out of the rock; and he rolled a stone against the door of the tomb.
>
> 47. Mary Magdalene and Mary the mother of Joses saw where he was laid.

The text links the narrative of the crucifixion (15.20–41) with that of the empty tomb (16.1–8). The note of time 'in the evening' (v.42) takes up the 'third hour' (15.25) when Jesus was crucified and the 'sixth to ninth hour' (15.33) during which time darkness fell. In other words, according to Mark, Jesus died around 3 o'clock in the afternoon (= the ninth hour); the burial took place in the evening.

There are two references to the crucifixion scene in v.44; the amazement of Pilate at Jesus' rapid death makes sense above all in the context of the Markan passion narrative, since according to that, against the rules, the time of Jesus' suffering was unusually short.[15] That is why Pilate was surprised. The scene is connected with what has gone before by the questioning of the centurion on duty (v.44; cf. v.39, the centurion under the cross). There are further links with the context in the fact that 15.36b and 16.3 correspond almost word for word and the women both stand under the cross and observe the burial from afar, and go to the empty tomb (15.40,47; 16.1).

The traditions in Mark 15.42–46

[42] The note of time 'and when evening had come' comes from Mark himself, like those in 4.35; 6.37; 14.17. However, there is probably a basis in tradition for the mention of the day of rest. Mark explains it for his readers as the day before the sabbath (cf. the similar explanation of Jewish customs in Mark 7.3f.).

[43] The characterization of Josephus as a '*respected* member of the council' hardly goes back to old tradition. For this description is urgently necessary only for Mark's conception: Joseph, a member of the Sanhedrin which condemned Jesus to death (Mark 14.55; 15.1), at the same time expected the kingdom of God. Here Mark, while not depicting Joseph as a Christian, does single him out from the group of Jesus' opponents. By this characterization, and given the quite positive significance that the 'kingdom of God' has in the Gospel of Mark (cf. 1.15), Joseph becomes a positive figure.

Certainly Mark would have preferred to relate a burial of Jesus by his followers, like the burial of John the Baptist (6.29). But as he had no tradition of this, and at the same time a report about the burial of Jesus by a member of the council, Joseph of Arimathea, was in circulation, he made the improvements to Joseph's character mentioned above. In that case the assumption that Joseph's membership of the Sanhedrin is part of the tradition has a good deal to be said for it, whereas his characterization as 'respected' comes from Mark himself.

[44–46] These verses were certainly composed by Mark himself. This is already suggested by the shift in the Greek terminology: in v.43 Joseph had asked for the *body* of Jesus; in v.45 Pilate gives him the *corpse* of Jesus. The two verses link the scene to what has gone before. The death of Jesus is real, and as it were officially confirmed.

[46] The statement of the burial of Jesus by Joseph is part of the tradition. The information about the rock tomb with a stone rolled in front of it already prepares for Mark 16.3 and was not originally part of the story. As this description of the tomb of Jesus is presupposed in Mark 16.1–8 (otherwise the story there would make no sense), whereas here at any rate it is an expansion, the mention of the rock tomb with the stone rolled in front of it may possibly have been taken over from there.

The shroud of (used) linen may be part of the tradition. It is customary in all forms of burial in Judaism. But it is striking that

Joseph *buys* linen. That implies that it is new. If we could say that the burial of Jesus by Joseph goes back to tradition, the new linen may represent a change to prevent any element of dishonour in the burial of Jesus.[16]

On the other hand, there are indications of deviations from the circumstances of a normal burial. Thus we must note that Jesus was certainly not buried in the family tomb in Nazareth, which would have been an essential feature of an honourable burial. Furthermore Mark had reported the anointing of Jesus *before* his death in ch.14 and understood it as an anointing for death. But there is no honourable anointing of the *body* of Jesus, as is known from the burial ritual elsewhere.

So the tradition in Mark 15.42–47 reports a burial of Jesus by Joseph of Arimathea, a member of the Sanhedrin. However, we cannot discover any more historical information about the nature of the burial from this narrative alone. Still, there are indications that Mark was confronted with the tradition of a dishonourable burial and reinterpreted this.

The revision of Mark 15.42–47 by Matthew and Luke

The parallels Matthew and Luke, and also John, have Christianized the figure of Joseph or drawn it in an even more positive way than Mark before them. Matthew differed from his Markan model by making Joseph of Arimathea a rich man and a disciple of Jesus (Matt.27.57). Luke portrays him as a good and just man (Luke 23.50) who took no part in the judgment by the Sanhedrin (Luke 23.51), and in Gospel of Peter[17] 6.23 he is called 'friend of the Lord'.

In John, too, Joseph of Arimathea is described as a disciple of Jesus (John 19.38), but he keeps this discipleship hidden for fear of the Jews (cf. John 12.42; 9.22). The narrative contains the further detail that Nicodemus, 'who had first (viz.John 3.2) come to Jesus by night' (19.39a), came to help Joseph prepare Jesus' body for burial (19.39f.).

The tendency in the early Christian narrative tradition of the burial of Jesus by Joseph of Arimathea should have become sufficiently clear. The counsellor has become a disciple of Jesus –

one could almost say that the foe has become a friend – and finally yet another friend of Jesus, Nicodemus, takes part in the burial.

But the burial, too, is painted in increasingly positive colours. Whereas Mark merely says that it was a rock tomb, the parallels not only presuppose this but also know that it was Joseph's own tomb (Matt.27.60; Gospel of Peter 6.24[18]). John (20.15) and Gospel of Peter 6.24 even locate it in the garden, which is a distinction (cf. II Kings 21.18,26). Finally, Matthew (27.60), Luke (23.53) and John (19.41f.) describe the tomb as new: this is a mark of honour for Jesus, and also excludes the possibility that Jesus was put, for example, in a criminal's grave.

We can now state that only Mark's account can serve as a source for the question of the historical value of the tradition. At the same time it should be noted that if the post-Markan tendency is to Christianize Joseph, my thesis that the Markan report probably already makes a positive change in the figure of Joseph is reinforced. If the story of the burial increasingly becomes a mark of honour for Jesus, is that not perhaps to displace a dishonourable burial? In other words, *is there not already in the Markan version a developed tradition which seeks to work over the terrible fact of Jesus' death to indicate that Jesus was at least given an orderly burial by a prominent counsellor?*

The account in John 19.31–37

John 19.31–37 is a further source for reconstructing the burial of Jesus:

31. Since it was the day of Preparation, in order to prevent the bodies from remaining on the cross on the sabbath (for that sabbath was a high day), the Jews asked Pilate that their legs might be broken, and that they might be taken away.
32. So the soldiers came and broke the legs of the first, and of the other who had been crucified with him;
33. but when they came to Jesus and saw that he was already dead, they did not break his legs.
34. But one of the soldiers pierced his side with a spear, and at once there came out blood and water.

35. He who saw it has borne witness – his testimony is true, and he knows that he tells the truth – that you also may believe.
36. For these things took place that the scripture might be fulfilled (Exod.12.46), 'Not a bone of him shall be broken.'
37. And again another scripture (Zech.12.10) says, 'They shall look on him whom they have pierced.'

The text is shaped in such a way as to translate Ps.34.21,[19] Exod.12.46 and Zech.12.10 into action (cf. the explicit phrase 'that the scripture should be fulfilled', v.36). But that does not prove that the whole narrative is a later invention. What remains as the core of the tradition is the request of the Jews for Jesus' body to be taken down from the cross (v.31). That this is an earlier tradition is indicated by the fact that the request was not granted. Why should anyone invent such a marginal note which plays no role in his literary plan?

Verse 38 begins all over again with Joseph's request, and he himself (not the Romans!) takes down the body from the cross. The incompatibility of the two accounts cannot be denied. Evidently the original conclusion of the narrative (the 'burial' of Jesus by James) has been removed. It was later replaced by the account of a burial of Jesus by Joseph and Nicodemus (John 19.38–42).

There is a parallel to what may be conjectured as the original note behind John 19.31–37 in Acts 13.29 (Jews 'took ... him [Jesus] down from the tree and laid him in the tomb'). Certainly it is often asserted that this verse is exclusively governed by Lukan language and theology and therefore comes from Luke himself. But that has by no means been proved. Normally Luke always lays the blame for the death of Jesus on the Jews in the mission speeches in Acts (2.23; 3.13–15; 4.27; 5.30; 7.52; 10.39; 13.28). But at this point (Acts 13.29) Jews see to taking the body away and to the burial, and that is hardly compatible with the motif of attaching blame. An interest in this course of action on Luke's part can hardly be explained. So this is an independent tradition which Luke took over and which corresponds to that behind John 19.31–37.

How Jesus really was buried

From the evidence that I have sketched out, in all probability we can conclude that the tradition of a burial of Jesus existed in two independent narratives: (a) Joseph of Arimathea asks Pilate for the body of Jesus and buries it; (b) Jews ask Pilate for the body of Jesus and bury it. *Here it is clear that tradition (b) will be the earlier one and (a) represents a later formation, at least as far as the tendencies towards a Christian interpretation indicated above are concerned.*

This raises the question how Jesus really was buried. First of all it must be explained how the burials of those who had been crucified were usually carried out at that time.

Roman legal practice provided for someone who died on the cross to rot there or to be consumed by vultures, jackals or other animals. This was to be a warning to the living. This possibility is excluded for Jesus, as the traditions agree in relating that his body was taken down from the cross (I Cor.15.4 also presupposes this). So the 'burial of Jesus' may be one of those cases in which the Roman authorities released the body. The Jewish writer Philo, at the beginning of the first century, reports such exceptions.[20] Presumably Jews took Jesus down from the cross, because someone who had died from crucifixion might not hang on the cross overnight (Deut.21.23) and because a feast day (= Passover) was imminent. Moreover the release of Jesus' body and its removal from the cross might also have suited Pilate, because this would *a priori* avoid unrest among the large numbers of visitors for the festival.

We can only conjecture the precise place of the burial of Jesus. The hypothesis that he was buried in the family tomb of Joseph of Arimathea comes to grief on the tendency of the early Christian accounts, which betray knowledge of a dishonourable burial of Jesus, or fear one. The assumption that Jesus was buried in a cemetery for those who had been executed, a Jewish practice, is almost impossible, because Jesus had not been executed by the Jewish authorities. As neither the disciples nor Jesus' next of kin bothered about Jesus' body, it is hardly conceivable that they were informed about its resting place.

The two strands of tradition reconstructed above perhaps agree in knowing Joseph of Arimathea. In that case he would have been the one who was charged (by the Jews) with seeing to the burial of Jesus. It is improbable that he was a disciple or a friend of Jesus. The opposite conclusion, that as a member of the Sanhedrin he was automatically one of Jesus' enemies, is equally improbable, since – historically speaking – there are serious doubts about a condemna-

tion of Jesus by the Supreme Council. We can no longer say where he (or unknown Jews) put the body.

Evidently not even the earliest community knew. For given the significance of tombs of saints in the time of Jesus, it can be presupposed that had Jesus' tomb been known, the early Christians would have venerated it, and traditions about it would have been preserved.[21]

The resurrection of Jesus

The real resurrection of Jesus from the dead, the event itself, is not described in any New Testament text. However, there are some texts outside the New Testament which describe the event of the resurrection itself. We shall see the context in which these traditions are to be put on pp.53ff. below.

In the formulation of statements about the resurrection of Jesus the resurrection appearance of Jesus to particular people is always already presupposed. For it was these appearances which first confirmed the notion that Jesus was risen. So the question of the resurrection appearances always plays a role in the question of the resurrection itself. Nevertheless, in faithfulness to the statements which Paul lists in I Cor.15, these will be treated separately later.

Here we shall now first of all consider a systematic analysis of the Easter stories in the four Gospels. The sequence in which they are treated (Mark, Luke, Matthew and John) follows from the date of the composition of the Gospels (for the chronological order see 7f. above). Here it should be stated *a priori* that each of the Gospels puts the accents differently in its account of the resurrection. Certainly in general we must presuppose that Mark underlies both the Gospels of Matthew and Luke and that in literary terms and in terms of tradition John is later. But 'we may not by any means understand this to indicate that the innovations in Matthew and Luke are simply the result of a literary revision of Mark or that the distinctive features of John are produced by a literary transformation of the synoptic texts. Behind the movement in the history of tradition attested by the texts there is a tradition which is both oral and written . . .'[22]

In 1971 the New Testament scholar Joachim Jeremias described the Easter accounts in the Gospels very precisely. He remarked that the most striking literary problem in the texts about the resurrection is their differences in detail and their colourful multiplicity. One can talk of a basic framework at most in the sequence of empty tomb and appearances. All the other statements in the text are very varied.

'This is true, first, of the people involved. The Risen One appears now to an individual, now to a couple of disciples, now to a small group, now to an enormous crowd. The witnesses are mostly men, but also women; they are members of the inmost group of disciples, other followers like Joseph and Matthias (cf. Acts 1.22f.), but also sceptics like the oldest of the family group, James (cf. I Cor.15.7), and at least in one case we have a fanatical opponent,'[23] namely Paul (I Cor.15.8).

Jeremias then refers to the various locations: in a house, in the open air, before the gates of Jerusalem, in a Judaean village, by the shore of Lake Gennesaret, in the hill-country of Galilee, once even outside Palestine, before Damascus.

This great divergence in the statements stands in crude opposition to the passion narratives in the Gospels. In the passion of Jesus the statements of the texts are almost uniform. According to Jeremias this structural difference between the account of the passion narrative and the Easter stories is grounded in the events themselves. For 'whereas the passion was an observable happening that took place in Jerusalem over the course of a few days, the Christophanies were a variety of events of different kinds which extended over a long period, probably over a number of years; the tradition limited the period of the Christophanies to forty days only at a relatively late stage (Acts 1.3)' (p.301).

Jeremias goes on to bring out three motifs which subsequently attached themselves to the Easter stories. First, people elaborated the reports of the appearances with words of the risen Jesus and conversations with him.

Secondly, the pressure of the burden of proof upon the first Christians influenced the final form of the Easter accounts. In the last resort they represented the reaction of the community to the doubt and mockery of outsiders (cf. the legend of the guards at the tomb in Matt.27.62–66; 28.11–15) and therefore also put particular emphasis on the bodily nature of the risen Christ (Luke 24.39; John 20.20; Luke 24.41–43).

Thirdly the development within the church shaped the Easter stories; thus church formulae (Matt.28.19), the church calendar (John 20.26; Acts 2.1ff.) and above all the missionary obligation of the church (Matt.28.16–20; Luke 24.44–49; Acts 1.4–8) have been worked into the accounts.

However, it is certain that something must have happened after Jesus' death which led his followers to speak of Jesus as the risen Christ. Many reactions to the resurrection of Jesus have been handed down in the New Testament, in part already from a very early period. They extend from brief statements of faith like 'God who has raised Jesus from the dead' to extended Easter stories. Only in the latter is there hope of finding an answer through critical analyses to the question what really happened historically at Easter.

The Easter event according to Mark

The original conclusion of the Gospel of Mark (Mark 16.1–8)

1. And when the sabbath was past, Mary Magdalene, and Mary the mother of James, and Salome, bought spices, so that they might go and anoint him.

2. And very early on the first day of the week they went to the tomb when the sun had risen.

3. And they were saying to one another, 'Who will roll away the stone for us from the door of the tomb?'

4. And looking up, they saw that the stone was rolled back; for it was very large.

5. And entering the tomb, they saw a young man sitting on the right side, dressed in a white robe; and they were amazed.

6. And he said to them, 'Do not be amazed; you seek Jesus of Nazareth, who was crucified. He has risen, he is not here; see the place where they laid him.

7. But go, tell his disciples and Peter that he is going before you to Galilee; there you will see him, as he told you.'

8. And they went out and fled from the tomb; for trembling and astonishment had come upon them; and they said nothing to any one, for they were afraid.

This report is remarkable in a number of ways: the first problem that it poses relates to its position at the end of the Gospel. It has been demonstrated and recognized that the following verses, from Mark 16.9 on, have been added only later. That raises the question: how can a Gospel have ended with the statement 'for they were afraid' (v.8)?

Attempts have long been made to reconstruct an original ending to the Gospel of Mark. It is pointed out that various conclusions were given to it in the second century and that the parallels Matthew and Luke supplemented the Mark that they had before them, which extended as far as 16.8. From this it is inferred that the original conclusion to Mark was broken off at a very early stage (through the loss of a page or by a deliberate excision). That would certainly remove the problem discussed here.

However, regardless of any supplements, for reasons of method we must first attempt to understand the Gospel of Mark as it has been handed down in its present form. Speculations about lost parts may only begin if there can be no agreed interpretation of the parts which are certainly authentic. Moreover it is often forgotten that if a page was lost, it must already have been lost from the very first copy. For books were constantly copied by scribes, and the later the damage was done in this process of copying, the more we would expect at least one instance of the original ending to Mark to have been preserved.

The second problem presented here lies in the content of what Mark reports. If the women did not obey the command of the angel, as v.8 says, how did the message of the resurrection then reach the disciples and Peter? So there may be something wrong historically here.

[1] The story is introduced by an indication of time ('sabbath' takes up 'day before the sabbath' [15.42]). The note of time in v.1 is then repeated once again in v.2 ('on the first day after the sabbath'). The date 'third day' presupposed here is certainly part of the tradition. Here we cannot exclude the possibility that the date was already meant to justify the church's festival of Easter (cf. Acts 20.7; Rev.1.10; I Cor.16.2 [?]).

The planned anointing recalls 14.3–9 (the anointing of Jesus by the [anonymous] woman[24] in Bethany). There it takes place in advance 'for the burial' (14.8). By again citing this motif here in

16.1 in connection with the women, Mark frames the account of the passion with narratives which have similar motifs.[25] Underlying this, however, could be the original tradition of a funeral lament by the women (cf. Luke 23.27).

The names of the women take up Mark 15.40 and 15.47. In all three cases Mary of Magdala appears at their head. Mark evidently thought that this was the same group around Mary. However, as so far there had been no mention of these women disciples of Jesus in the Gospel, he adds in 15.41 that they had already followed Jesus at an early stage in Galilee and served him (cf. Mark 1.31).

Here we need to ask whether the multiple mention of the women goes back to different traditions. If this could be demonstrated, we would have all the more reason to assume that the basis of this was a group of people who were generally known at the time.

15.40f. gives the impression of being isolated in its context. The confession of the centurion under the cross, 'Truly this man was the Son of God' (15.39), is the climax, and the list of women (15.40) with an explanation (15.41) looks like a supplement. Now Mark himself certainly formulated v.41. The mention of the three women by name in Mark 15.40 ('Mary of Magdala and Mary the mother of James the younger and of Joses and of Salome') agrees with Mark 16.1 and 15.47: Mary of Magdala, Mary and Salome. By contrast, the surnames of the Maries differ in 15.47 ('the mother of Joses') and 16.1 ('the mother of James'), which might indicate independent traditions; however, each time they agree with one surname of Mary from Mark 15.40. So it may be assumed that Mark himself also constructed this v.40, by taking over the names of the women from the traditions of Mark 16.1 and 15.47.

At the same time it may be doubted whether the women from 15.47 were originally associated with the burial of Jesus. Rather, Mark found their names in his tradition of the passion and moved them to this point in order to create a better transition to 16.1.

So we can affirm that women were mentioned both in the passion narrative and in the subsequent story of the visit to the tomb, independently of one another.

[2] 'Tomb' relates back to the same word in 15.46. 'When the

sun had risen' connects with 'when evening had come' (15.42): nightfall had prevented the anointing of Jesus. That one could not buy unguents in the morning before sunrise does not disturb the narrator. The all-important thing is for the women to get to the tomb.

[3–4] 'Stone' and 'door of the tomb' pick up the same words from 15.46. Mark himself probably elaborated this verse, like the next.

[5] The young man in the white garment[26] is a heavenly figure. Matthew 28.2 later specifically identifies him as an angel.

The whole event is a kind of appearance scene. 'Sitting on the right' gives the message of the young man emphasis and confirms it, as 'right' indicates the correct, happy side (cf. John 21.6, etc.) and 'sit' evidently expresses the authority with which the young man speaks (cf. Dan.7.9; Rev.21.5).

The reaction of the women, their amazement (not at the empty tomb but at the angel), has features of Markan language: thus the term used here for 'amazed' occurs only in Mark in the New Testament (9.15; 14.33; 16.56). This is a Markan word which leads to the theme of the suffering Christ that will stand in the foreground until Mark 16.8.

[6] 'Amazed' takes up the same word from v.5. 'Jesus of Nazareth, who was crucified' is a later insertion and refers back to the passion narrative (Mark 14–15) and to the predictions of the passion (Mark 8.31; 9.31; 10.34). The addition 'of Nazareth' (cf. 1.24; 10.47; 14.67) makes the identification with the earthly Jesus certain.

The message of the young man is that Jesus has been raised. It corresponds to Jesus' own prediction in 8.31; 9.31; 10.34. The reference to the empty tomb ('he is not here') underlines the reality of the resurrection of Jesus. But here the sequence must be noted: first comes the statement 'Jesus has been raised'; 'only then does the empty tomb come into view: Jesus has been raised – he is not here – so the tomb is empty'.[27]

[7] The verse contains the charge to the women to tell the disciples and Peter that Jesus will go before them into Galilee. This is an explicit reference back to Mark 14.28 ('But after I am raised up, I will go before you into Galilee'); it is obvious that both verses are later constructions. The Gospel is to end where it began: in Galilee. Here, as in Mark 10.32, Jesus' going before

refers to the Christian way, which is to be taken in discipleship of Jesus. Here Mark stands in the earliest Christian tradition, in which the 'way' has become a technical term for the 'Christian way' (cf. Acts 9.2: 'followers of the new way').

[8] The flight of the women recalls the flight of the disciples in 14.50. Their flight is described twice in the present verse (cf. the similar duplication in Mark 10.32). It leads to their telling no one anything, contrary to the express command of the young man. This disobedience is matched by the failure of the disciples throughout the Gospel of Mark.

The sentence 'for they were afraid' which concludes the Gospel comes from Mark. As the end of a narrative and a gospel it is certainly unusual and surprising, but quite conceivable. Reference need be made only to Gen.18.15 in the version of the Greek translation ('Then Sarah denied it and said, "I did not laugh" – for she was afraid') as evidence that 'they were afraid' could stand at the end of a sentence and a story. Moreover v.8b is a reference back to the fear of the women, which has been depicted in a vivid way. So 'it is hard to dispute that the text as it stands is probably understandable and displays an effective rhythm'.[28]

The abrupt concluding verse Mark 16.8 fits very well into the conception of the Gospel of Mark: if the women are silent, everything that follows depends on Jesus' showing himself in the Christian community. And this is of great interest for Mark's plan.

Mark 16.1–8 is thus a meaningful end to the Gospel, in the way in which it vividly illustrates the kerygma of the cross and resurrection (v.6) that has been clad in the dramatic episode 16.1–8. Similarly, the whole Gospel can be understood as a vivid presentation of this message (= proclamation as narrative).

The tradition behind Mark 16.1–8 and its historical content

Now that the textual basis for the story of the resurrection in Mark 16.1–8 has been established, in what follows we shall be concerned with the traditions behind it and the question of their historicity. I have already commented that the mention of the women (Mary Magdalene, Mary Salome) was not first worked into the story of the visit to the tomb by Mark but already belonged to it in the tradition.

Next, we must clarify whether Mark 16.1–8*[29] was part of a longer pre-Markan passion story.

The following reasons tell against Mark 16.1–8* being an element of a pre-Markan passion story and for the text as being an originally independent unit:

1. Mark 16.1 is a new beginning.

2. In Mark 16.1 and 15.47 there are two different lists of women. Had both texts belonged together, probably only one list would have been handed down.

3. References to the Old Testament, which are frequent in the passion narrative elsewhere, are absent from Mark 16.1–8.

4. Mark 16.1–8 and the story of the burial in Mark 15.42–47 do not fit together well. In the story of the burial, the burial of Jesus seems complete. Furthermore, the intention of the women to anoint the body on Easter morning (Mark 16.1) is in conflict with this, since such a plan presupposes that the body has not been anointed and therefore that the burial is only provisional.

So it may be regarded as probable that Mark 16.1–8* was not an ingredient of a pre-Markan passion narrative, but a small independent unit which Mark worked in at this point.

The expressiveness of the narrative is also remarkable. Rudolf Bultmann describes the structure of the story as 'impressive: the wondering of the women, i.e., the sight of the rolled-away stone and the appearance of the angel, vv.4f., the masterly formulated angelic message v.6 and the shattering impression in v.8'[30] which is given by the discovery of the empty tomb. Of course interest grew on both sides (both Christians and their opponents) in the resting-place of the body of Jesus, especially as a proclamation of Jesus as the risen Christ provocatively posed to both opponents and unbelievers the question of what happened to Jesus' corpse. Matthew 28.13–15 is impressive evidence of this situation:

13. Tell people, 'His disciples came by in the night and stole him away while we were asleep.'
. . .
15. So they took the money and did as they were directed; and this story has been spread among the Jews to this day.

Thus the narrative of Mark 16.1–8 serves a twofold purpose: it combines the Christian preaching of the resurrection of Jesus with its consequence, the empty tomb. *However, it cannot be used as evidence that the tomb was in fact empty. The aim of the narrative is to provide arguments against possible criticism: vv.3–6 defend the fact of the resurrection and v.8 the authenticity of what is reported.*

Only the statements of Mark 16.1–8 allow an attempt to reconstruct the origin of the tradition. At the beginning stood the message of the resurrection (v.6). From it developed the story of the empty tomb as a defence against polemical questions from opponents of early Christianity. It was not strange that women were the main figures in this legend, since the flight of the disciples was known; so they could not be used as witnesses to the resurrection. But at the same time the women were part of the passion narrative, and so because of the link between passion, death and resurrection in Christian proclamation a need may have been felt also to tell of how they came to hear of the resurrection of Jesus. So subsequently, on the basis of early Christian faith, a legend was formed with women as those who received the proclamation of the resurrection at Jesus' tomb.

That the 'creed' of the death and resurrection of Jesus – combined with an appearance to Peter – stood at the beginning of this development follows indirectly from v.7. Here 'the disciples and Peter' appear in connection with 'seeing' the risen Lord. That may relate to the old tradition in I Cor.15.5 in which Cephas and the twelve were mentioned as the first witnesses to the appearance of the Risen Christ. (Note that v.7 has been inserted by Mark into the tradition, but earlier knowledge seems to have been preserved in his statement.)

The journey of Mary Magdalene and the two other women to the tomb of Jesus on the day after the sabbath can hardly be said to be historical. The source is a legend which arose at a late stage, directed against attacks from opponents, and could not have existed without a 'Christian' faith which was present earlier. For it was 'concluded' that the tomb of Jesus was empty only from the message that the one who had been crucified had been raised. The existing story is so to speak the product of an inference. The story is first inferred from the 'dogma'. In all honesty, nothing can be derived from this as to what really happened historically.

The later ending to the Gospel of Mark (Mark 16.9–20)

9. Now when he rose early on the first day of the week, he appeared first to Mary Magdalene, from whom he had cast out seven demons.

10. She went and told those who had been with him, as they mourned and wept.

11. But when they heard that he was alive and had been seen by her, they would not believe it.

12. After this he appeared in another form to two of them, as they were walking into the country.

13. And they went back and told the rest, but they did not believe them.

14. Afterward he appeared to the eleven themselves as they sat at table; and he upbraided them for their unbelief and hardness of heart, because they had not believed those who saw him after he had risen.

15. And he said to them, 'Go into all the world and preach the gospel to the whole creation.

16. He who believes and is baptized will be saved; but he who does not believe will be condemned.

17. And these signs will accompany those who believe: in my name they will cast out demons; they will speak in new tongues;

18. they will pick up serpents, and if they drink any deadly thing, it will not hurt them; they will lay their hands on the sick, and they will recover.'

19. So then the Lord Jesus, after he had spoken to them, was taken up into heaven, and sat down at the right hand of God.

20. And they went forth and preached everywhere, while the Lord worked with them and confirmed the message by the signs that attended it.

The text shows some special features: it presupposes a first appearance to Mary Magdalene, thus probably suppressing the first appearance to Cephas. But at the same time the significance of the appearance to Mary is weakened: certainly she appears at the head of a chain of witnesses, but all the emphasis is put on the later appearance to the eleven disciples, to whom the instructions of Jesus, related in detail, apply (vv.15–18).

The motif of unbelief runs through the section (vv.11,13,14).

At the same time there is a summons to faith (the right faith, vv.16,17). Thus the text is to be seen as a defence of belief in the resurrection, at the same time referring to the miracle of the church (v.18).[31]

The passage was certainly not just composed specially as an ending to the Gospel of Mark, but already existed beforehand, probably as a kind of 'Easter catechism in community instruction'.[32] *It is a kind of summary of the Easter reports known to the author.* However, no knowledge of the Gospels of Mark and Matthew can be demonstrated here, though there is clearly knowledge of the Gospels of Luke and John, and of Acts.[33] *No further insights can be derived from Mark 16.9–20 in addition to the evidence that can be ascertained there.*

The Easter event according to Luke

Luke writes that 'many have already undertaken to compile a narrative of the things which have been accomplished among us' (1.1) and describes them as 'eye-witnesses and ministers of the word' (1.2). Two of the sources which Luke presupposes here are well known, the Gospel of Mark and Q, though he never mentions them explicitly (see above, 7ff.).

As becomes clear in the foreword to Luke's Gospel, the idea of the fulfilment of scripture dominates Luke-Acts – the reference is to the 'prophecies' of the Old Testament. Luke's main theological concern is thus to demonstrate that the prophecies of the Old Testament have been fulfilled by the activity of Jesus. Of course the scene of this event must be the 'holy city' of Jerusalem.

This concern also stands in the foreground of Luke 24, the chapter on the resurrection. In addition Luke seems to have had an interest in the bodily resurrection of Jesus, in order to refute different claims which disparaged the Christians and their faith (see below, 44ff.).

The empty tomb and the announcement of the resurrection of Jesus (Luke 24.1–12)

1. But on the first day of the week, at early dawn, they went to the tomb, taking the spices which they had prepared.
2. And they found the stone rolled away from the tomb,

3. but when they went in they did not find the body.

4. While they were perplexed about this, behold, two men stood by them in dazzling apparel;

5. and as they were frightened and bowed their faces to the ground, the men said to them, 'Why do you seek the living among the dead?

6. Remember how he told you, while he was still in Galilee,

7. that the Son of man must be delivered into the hands of sinful men, and be crucified, and on the third day rise.'

8. And they remembered his words,

9. and returning from the tomb they told all this to the eleven and to all the rest.

10. Now it was Mary Magdalene and Joanna and Mary the mother of James and the other women with them who told this to the apostles;

11. but these words seemed to them an idle tale, and they did not believe them.

12. But Peter rose and ran to the tomb: stooping and looking in, he saw the linen cloths by themselves; and he went home wondering at what had happened.

The Lukan significance of the story and its sources can best be discovered from a comparison with Mark, on which it is based. Small details apart, the text differs from it at the following points:

1. The women saw the tomb of Jesus (Luke 23.55) and prepared spices and oil for anointing the evening before. They rested during the ensuing sabbath in accordance with the commandment (Luke 23.56). In Mark the women only saw (from afar) where the body of Jesus had been laid (15.47). They bought spices to anoint the body *after* the sabbath (Mark 16.1). Luke 24.1 does not explicitly mention the intention to anoint the body. 'Since according to Luke the women had already prepared their spices on the day of the burial, they can hasten to the tomb even earlier. Their coming as early as possible in the morning attests the magnitude of their love and worship.'[34]

2. The names of the women are mentioned by Luke only at the end of the story (v.10), by Mark already at the beginning (v.1).[35] The names of two women agree: Mary Magdalene and Mary the mother of James. Salome (Mark 16.1) does not appear in Luke, but Joanna does; she had already been mentioned in Luke 8.3 as

the wife of Chuza. That is probably why Luke himself mentions her here again. In addition Luke mentions the other women who had accompanied Jesus – here, too, he is probably thinking of Luke 8.2–3.

3. In Luke the women do not worry about who will roll away the stone for them (Mark 16.3 differs), but, as in the Markan account, they find the stone rolled away from the tomb and enter it (Mark 16.4/Luke 24.2f.).

4. The next remark, 'they did not find the body of Jesus', has no parallel in Mark. There it is the young man, having given his message of the resurrection, who first points to the empty tomb. This shift of accent, along with the observation that Luke 24.3 explicitly mentions the body of Jesus (see above, Luke 23.55), indicates a stronger emphasis on the empty tomb and the bodily resurrection.

5. In Luke two men meet the women (in Mark a young man [16.5]), in dazzling apparel (Luke 24.4); they recall the 'two men in white garments' in the scene of the ascension in Acts 1.10 (cf. Luke 9.30,32).

6. The message of the young man in Mark (16.6) ran: 'You seek Jesus of Nazareth, who was crucified. He has risen, he is not here; see the place where they laid him' (16.6). In Luke 24.5b–6a this becomes: 'Why do you seek the living among the dead? He is not here, but has been raised.' Thus the women are chided – why are they coming to seek Jesus here anyway?

7. Luke 24.6b–8 differs considerably from Mark 16.7. In Mark (and similarly Matt.28.7) the women are charged to tell Jesus' disciples and Peter that they are to go to Galilee, where they will see Jesus, as it has been told them. By contrast, in Luke, in Lukan language (e.g. 'into the hands of sinful men' [v.7]), the two men refer the women back to the message of Jesus which they had been given earlier in Galilee, that the Son of Man had to suffer and rise again on the third day (Luke 9.22; cf. 9.44; 18.32f.). Hence the reproach in v.6, for this prophecy of the resurrection must have been known to them. For them to forget it or not to heed it meant an absence of faith.

8. In Mark the women are silent despite the charge to them; in Luke they pass on to the eleven disciples (Judas no longer counts in the group of twelve) and all the rest the message of the resurrection without having to be told to do so (v.9), but meet

with unbelief (v.11). However, the role of the women as those who proclaim the Easter message is not played down by this. For in contrast to the account in Mark, the women are portrayed positively, and it is the apostles (vv.10f.) who do not believe, not the women.

9. Mark, on which Luke is based, knows nothing of a visit of Peter to the tomb (Luke 24.12). Here there is a tension with the subsequent text: Luke 24.24 says that 'some' went to the tomb. These tensions can be explained by the use of an existing tradition which Luke inserted here. That he himself created the transitions is clear from the Lukan language in v.12: 'rise', 'wonder', 'what had happened'.[36]

The question arises as to where Luke (or his source) got the report of a visit of Peter to the tomb from. The following answer suggests itself: Luke (or his tradition) knew the tradition of an appearance of Jesus to Peter (cf. Luke 24.34) and also the tradition of a visit of the women to the tomb. Both are combined in Luke 24.12, and added where they belong, namely at the end of the women's visit to the tomb. The author's idea could then have been that if the women reported that the tomb was empty and if Jesus appeared to Cephas, he must himself have been convinced of the empty tomb and therefore must have gone there. Either Luke himself or, more probably, the tradition which he used will have been the author of this combination.

Now there is a parallel to Peter's visit to the tomb in John 20.3–8. Either this passage presupposes a knowledge of Luke 24.12, or Luke and John are using a tradition of this visit to the tomb which is known to both of them. Because of the striking common linguistic features, it is certain that the two passages belong together. But in any case the tradition which appears in Luke 24.12 is primarily a development of the tradition about the tomb in Mark 16.1–8 using the tradition of a first appearance to Peter. *So the tradition behind Luke 24.12 is a later construction and therefore without historical value for the question of the 'resurrection events'.*

The encounter with the disciples on the Emmaus road (Luke 24.13–35)

The present narrative consists of four sections:

13–16: Introduction: two disciples meet Jesus on the road from Jerusalem to Emmaus;

17–27: Conversation on the way;

28–31: Meal scene;

32–35: Return from Emmaus to Jerusalem.

13. That very day two of them were going to a village named Emmaus, about seven miles from Jerusalem,

14. and talking with each other about all these things that had happened.

15. While they were talking and discussing together, Jesus himself drew near and went with them.

16. But their eyes were kept from recognizing him.

17. And he said to them, 'What is this conversation which you are holding with each other as you walk?', and they stood still, looking sad.

18. Then one of them, named Cleopas, answered him, 'Are you the only visitor to Jerusalem who does not know the things that have happened there in these days?'

19. And he said to them, 'What things?' And they said to him, 'Concerning Jesus of Nazareth, who was a prophet mighty in deed and word before God and all the people,

20. and how our chief priests and rulers delivered him up to be condemned to death, and crucified him.

21. But we had hoped that he was the one to redeem Israel. Yes, and besides all this, it is now the third day since this happened.

22. Moreover, some women of our company amazed us. They were at the tomb early in the morning

23. and did not find his body; and they came back saying that they had even seen a vision of angels, who said that he was alive.

24. Some of those who were with us went to the tomb, and found it just as the women had said; but him they did not see.'

25. And he said to them, 'O foolish men, and slow of heart to believe all that the prophets have spoken!

26. Was it not necessary that the Christ should suffer these things and enter into his glory?'

27. And beginning with Moses and all the prophets, he interpreted to them in all the scriptures the things concerning himself.

28. So they drew near to the village to which they were going. He appeared to be going further,

29. but they constrained him, saying, 'Stay with us, for it is toward evening and the day is now far spent.' So he went in to stay with them.

30. When he was at table with them, he took the bread and blessed, and broke it, and gave it to them.

31. And their eyes were opened and they recognized him; and he vanished out of their sight.

32. They said to each other, 'Did not our hearts burn within us while he talked to us on the road, while he opened to us the scriptures?'

33. And they rose that same hour and returned to Jerusalem; and they found the eleven gathered together and those who were with them,

34. who said, 'The Lord has risen indeed, and has appeared to Simon!'

35. Then they told what had happened on the road, and how he was known to them in the breaking of the bread.

A. Introduction (Luke 24.13–16)

[13] 'And behold' is a Lukan introduction (see most recently 23.50); 'of them' links the narrative with what has gone before; 'that very day' comes from Luke; according to Luke all the resurrection scenes take place on one and the same day.

[14] This refers back to v.9, in which the women reported 'all these things'; the disciples did not believe them (v.11) and Peter inspected the tomb nevertheless.

[15] The two disciples, too, whose names are not yet mentioned, cannot leave the report alone: they discuss it (cf. Luke 22.23 with Acts 6.9). The sequel picks this up: Jesus joins them and travels on with them.

[16] Their eyes were kept from recognizing him right at the beginning of the encounter.

That is the end of the introduction. The 'resolution' will consist in their eyes being opened (v.31). But before that can happen the two, and thus the readers, are to undergo a recognition process. This begins with the conversation on the way in vv.17–27.

B. *The conversation on the way (Luke 24.17–27)*

[17–19] Jesus begins – in real Lukan fashion (cf. Acts 8.30; 9.4,10, etc.) – with a question which opens the dialogue. The noting of their sorrow is emphasized by the pause in the external scene (they remain at a standstill) which heightens the tension. In the twofold exchange of a question from Jesus (v.17) and a more allusive counter-question from a disciple (Cleopas, v.18) expressing a reproach, a further question from Jesus and a first brief piece of information (v.19), it finally becomes clear that they are talking about Jesus himself, who is termed a 'prophet, mighty in deed and word before God and all the people'.

Verse 19 is completely shaped by Luke. Only he uses the Greek word for 'before' which appears here (Luke 1.6; 20.26; Acts 7.10; 8.32 [= Isa.53.7]). The people often calls Jesus 'prophet' (Luke 16; 9.8,19 and indirectly Luke 7.39). But it has to be asked why the two disciples also call Jesus a prophet here. This does not happen elsewhere in Luke. The answer lies in the failure of the disciples to recognize Jesus: they do not recognize Jesus and thus at the same time cannot understand his role as Messiah and Son of God. The recognition of Jesus later turns into the recognition of the role of Jesus (v.26). So v.19 produces a tension (like v.18 before it) which looks for resolution.

[20] This describes the death of Jesus in a Lukan way: the *Jews* crucified Jesus (cf. Acts 7.51–53 and the exoneration of Pilate in the Lukan passion narrative, where he washes his hands in innocence).

[21] This points back to the original but disappointed hope of the disciples that Jesus would redeem Israel with his power (cf. Luke 1.68; 2.38; Acts 1.6). Thus they largely begin from the role of Jesus as the Jewish Messiah. The Christian image of the Messiah redeeming everyone (not a people!) by his suffering and weakness does not yet occur to them. But at the time of Luke this purely Jewish hope has been long superseded by the creation of a church of the Gentiles (the achievement of Paul – see the end of Acts).

With 'third day' (see below, 49f.), Luke refers back to the point in time of the Easter stories and in vv.22–24 sums up what is known so far.

[22] This links up with the story of the visit of the women to the tomb which has been told previously.

[23] This repeats their vision of the angel and the message to them that Jesus is alive.

[24] This refers back to v.12, where the word 'some' generalizes the visit of an individual, Peter.

[25] This indicates that the previous faith of the disciples is insufficient and introduces the new (correct) knowledge of the role of Jesus – first of all through a reproach from Jesus (which is similar to the reproach to the women in Luke 24.5–8).

[26] This characterizes the suffering of Christ as necessary and in accordance with the scriptures (v.27; cf. v.25). It is wholly in accord with the Lukan notion of salvation history (cf. Luke 24.6b,44), the course of which is thought of as being necessary in all its elements.[37] Here Luke puts particular emphasis on the paradoxical discovery that the suffering and death of Jesus do not mean a failure but his victory: the Christ destined for glory *had to* suffer. This notion was inconceivable for Jews.

[27] This expresses the general Lukan conviction that Christ is mentioned in the books of Moses and in the Prophets (cf. Acts 8.35), but does not produce any quotations to attest this.

C. *The meal (vv.28–31)*

[28] The destination has almost been reached. Jesus' intention to go on increases the tension. – The Lord wants to be asked, and then it is certain that he will stay. Now, where everything is moving towards the climax, i.e. the recognition of Jesus by the two disciples, Jesus cannot just go on and disappear.

[29] The two disciples urgently ask Jesus to stay (cf. Rev.3.20). 'What is formally meant on their lips as an invitation imperceptibly becomes – so the reader must judge – a prayer to the Kyrios Jesus, "Stay with us, for it is towards evening and the day is now far spent." This subtle irony is theologically quite appropriate: it matches the conduct of the risen Jesus. The traveller accedes to the disciples' request and goes with them into the house, "to stay with them", as it is said, not without further connotations.'[38]

[30] Jesus breaks bread at the common meal, blesses it and gives it to them. The many verbal allusions to the eucharistic words in Luke 22.19 from v.30 on indicate that here Luke is thinking in terms of the eucharist.

[31] Their eyes are opened and they recognize him – as a person

and as 'Christian Messiah'. Thus their 'blindness' of v.16 is removed. What Luke wants to convey is that communion with Jesus is experienced in the eucharist. Once that is clear, all has been said: Jesus can now vanish – but he will always be there. This explicit statement that the one who appears vanishes is typically Lukan: Luke 1.38; 2.15; 9,33; Acts 10.7; 12.10.

D. *The return from Emmaus to Jerusalem (vv.32–35)*

[32] In retrospect the disciples recognize that their hearts were already burning within them when Jesus interpreted the old prophecies to them on the way. Even there the longing for Jesus as the true Christ was unconsciously aroused in them.

[33] Now the two disciples can return to Jerusalem, to the rest (as the women did in v.9).

[34] Before the two disciples can communicate the knowledge that they have just gained, the eleven disciples tell them of an appearance of Jesus to Peter. This spoils their story. Here, as in other passages (Acts 8.14ff.; 11.1,22), Luke makes room for a Jerusalem perspective. For him Jerusalem represents the centre, and everything must start here. So at this point he corrects his tradition and establishes that the first appearance was to Peter (in Jerusalem).[39] Later in Acts Luke will in fact portray Peter as leader of the earliest community (cf. Acts 2.14–20; 3.12–26) and the Jerusalem church as the earliest community of which the Lukan community is a descendant.

Here Luke wants to convey that the experience of the presence of Jesus which both the disciples on the road to Emmaus and all the members of his community have at the eucharist is confirmed by the earliest Christian confession: Jesus is truly risen and has appeared to Simon. In other words, all the other Easter experiences rest on this earliest Christian confession of faith.

[35] This sums up Luke's understanding once again: the two disciples relate what has happened to them on the way (including the fact that the prophecies have been explained to them and how this was done) and that they recognized Jesus in the breaking of the bread.

What has been said so far has shown that the Emmaus story represents a self-contained unit which at every point is permeated by

Luke's theological conception. Although it is certain that Luke has worked on material which was already in existence, a reconstruction of the tradition which he used faces great difficulties.

As a test one could take out all the references to the Emmaus story proper to see whether the result provides the basic features of a tradition. What is left is a story which as early as 1903 Hermann Gunkel described like this: 'Here Christ appears unknown, as a wanderer – the role that the deity loved from of old, in simple human form, for example clad as a traveller to wander among human beings – and reveals his mysterious divine being at particular points; but as soon as he is recognized, he disappears. This outline of the story is very similar to the *earliest narratives about the appearance of the deity*; in style the story could be put in Genesis.'[40]

If we presuppose such a legend as the earliest stratum, we could distinguish from it the eucharistic tradition in vv.28–31, which may have been added at a second stage.

At the end of the analysis of the Emmaus story it should be emphasized that a purely historical enquiry produces only meagre results. So from the Emmaus story proper we can learn almost nothing in terms of historical detail, but something about the general character of Christian faith.

However, with due caution we can draw a few sparse conclusions: v.34 emphasizes the appearance to Simon (= Peter = Cephas) which is said by Paul in I Cor.15 to be the first appearance of the risen Christ. It is to be dated shortly after Jesus' death (around 30). We shall be returning to this later (83ff.).

Individual elements of the narrative are beyond doubt old: thus possibly behind the name Cleopas (v.18) lies Jesus' cousin Clopas,[41] whose son Symeon succeeded James as leader of the earliest community in 62.[42] In that case, in this story we would have a recollection of an appearance of Jesus to one of his relatives, which might go back to the earliest period. The name of the second traveller is not given.

The place Emmaus might also derive from historical knowledge, but its location is completely uncertain.

Jesus' appearance to the (eleven) disciples (Luke 24.36–53)

This section consists of three parts:

vv.36–43: Recognition scene (= narrative)

vv.44–49: Instruction of the disciples (= words of Jesus)
vv.50–53: Farewell (= narrative)

36. As they were saying this, Jesus himself stood among them.
37. But they were startled and frightened, and supposed that they saw a spirit.
38. And he said to them, 'Why are you troubled, and why do questionings rise in your hearts?
39. See my hands and my feet, that it is I myself; handle me, and see; for a spirit has not flesh and bones as you see that I have.'
40. And when he had said this, he showed them his hands and his feet.
41. And while they still disbelieved for joy, and wondered, he said to them, 'Have you anything here to eat?'
42. They gave him a piece of broiled fish,
43. and he took it and ate before them.

44. Then he said to them, 'These are my words which I spoke to you, while I was still with you, that everything written about me in the law of Moses and the prophets and the psalms must be fulfilled.'
45. Then he opened their minds to understand the scriptures,
46. and said to them, 'Thus it is written, that the Christ should suffer and on the third day rise from the dead,
47. and that repentance and forgiveness of sins should be preached in his name to all nations, beginning from Jerusalem.
48. You are witnesses to these things.
49. And behold, I send the promise of my Father upon you; but stay in the city, until you are clothed with power from on high.'

50. Then he led them out as far as Bethany, and lifting up his hands he blessed them.
51. While he blessed them, he parted from them.
52. And they returned to Jerusalem with great joy,
53. and were continually in the temple blessing God.

A. Recognition scene (Luke 24.36–43)

[36] 'As they were saying this' is a Lukan link between what follows and the previous scene; 'he stood among them' is also Lukan in language.

[37–38] 'But they were startled and frightened', 'see' and 'Spirit' (for the content see similarly Acts 12.8f.) derive from Luke, as does 'in your hearts'.

[39] With Jesus' invitation to the disciples to see his hands and his feet in order to recognize his identity, this gives a first demonstration (whether the disciples did this is not said, but is presupposed); the invitation to touch him and see is the second demonstration of the resurrection of Jesus. This refutes the fear mentioned in v.37 that he is a spirit: the risen Christ consists of flesh and blood. Evidently in this verse Luke is combatting challenges to the bodily reality of Jesus, as Ignatius, To the Smyrnaeans 3.2, does at the beginning of the second century:

> For I know and believe that he (viz. Jesus) was in the flesh even after the resurrection. And when he came to those with Peter he said to them: 'Take, handle me and see that I am not a phantom without a body.' And they immediately touched him and believed, being mingled both with his flesh and spirit.

[40] This is a variation on and intensification of v.39. It probably comes in its entirety from Luke.

[41–43] The introduction 'And while they' in v.41 corresponds to that in v.36 and comes from Luke. The disciples have already almost been convinced by Jesus. The third demonstration which now follows is meant to remove any doubt: eating broiled fish (v.42) proves that he cannot be either a spirit or an angel. Angels do not eat (cf. Tobit 12.19); human beings do. The narrator so much takes the probative force of this last demonstration for granted that he does not even have to emphasize that the disciples are convinced. Later Acts 1.4; 10.41 says that Jesus ate with his disciples. By stressing the physical reality of the risen Jesus, Luke evidently wants to strengthen the certainty of his readers.

That the whole scene cannot just come from Luke but follows a tradition is shown, first, by the tensions with the preceding Emmaus story: the disciples are afraid despite the previous encounter with the Emmaus road disciples and with Jesus. Here Luke would certainly have made a more skilful transition. Secondly, this is shown by the parallel tradition in Ignatius, To the Smyrnaeans 3.2 (see the comment on v.39).[43] The two texts may have arisen independently. For the statement 'I am not a phantom without a body' which is central in Ignatius must have come from the account on which he bases his remarks. However, it does not appear in Luke.

At the same time this suggests that in shaping Luke 24.36–43 Luke could in fact refer back to an already existing tradition. This consisted of the story of an appearance in which the risen Jesus appeared to his anxious disciples in bodily form. The central statement is the real bodily form of Jesus after the resurrection. The occasion for the formation of this tradition was probably a discussion within a community about the nature of the corporeality of the risen Christ of the kind that we find in the Johannine communities (cf. John 20; I John) and in its beginnings also already in the Pauline community of Corinth (I Cor.15). Accordingly this is a later formation – probably from the second generation, which no longer had any connection with the real witnesses to the 'resurrection of Jesus' and attempted to solve this riddle itself. What has emerged is a well-thought-out composition which in three progressive steps documents for the disciples the bodily nature of the risen Christ.

For these reasons it should have become clear that there is no relationship to the real testimony to the 'resurrection' of Jesus. The historical yield is virtually nil. This also applies to the whole section Luke 24.36–53, especially as at the same time it will become clear that the following verses are shaped through and through by the scheme of Luke's work and his theology.

B. *Instruction of the disciples (Luke 24.44–49)*

The whole section is a composition of Luke's which here, at the end of his Gospel, sums up the story of the resurrection once again and looks forward to the future, i.e. to his own day:

[44] Jesus refers in retrospect to what he has said to the disciples. The main content is explained further by the second part of the verse: as already during his lifetime, Jesus shows that the old prophecies have to be fulfilled.

[45] Jesus shows the disciples the meaning of the Old Testament scriptures as he already did in the Emmaus story (cf. esp.v.27). For this purpose he goes on to cite a so-called 'proof from scripture'.

[46] This verse corresponds to Luke 9.22, Jesus' prophecy that he would suffer and rise again on the third day.

[47] This directs attention towards the future and the task of the disciples. Part of the proof from scripture is that in Jesus' name 'repentance and forgiveness of sins should be preached in his name to all nations, beginning from Jerusalem' (cf. Acts 2.32f.,38; 3.15f.,9; 5.28–32; 10.39,43).

[48] This is ño longer part of the proof from scripture. Here Jesus addresses the disciples directly as witnesses to 'these things', i.e. as eye-witnesses to the passion and resurrection (cf. Acts 1.22).

[49] This corresponds to Acts 1.4. The prophecy about receiving the Spirit is later fulfilled in Acts 2.

C. Farewell (Luke 24.50–53)

The concluding account of the ascension likewise derives in its entirety from Luke. The section has a parallel in Acts 1.9–11, where the ascension takes place from the Mount of Olives (v.12); here by contrast it is from Bethany (v.50). However, that need not necessarily mean that the two scenes could be based on rival traditions. Luke knows from Mark 11.1 that the 'Mount of Olives' and 'Bethany' are geographically close together or are identical as place names. So here we could have a variation on one and the same place.

[51] For the disappearance of Jesus see the comments on Luke 24.31 (see pp.41f.). The concluding 'and was carried up to heaven' is in tension with the account in Acts, which in Acts 1.44ff. similarly reports an ascension of Jesus. Probably for that reason some manuscripts omit this statement, to harmonize between Acts 1.9 and Luke 24.51. However, if one reflects that Acts was probably written only ten years after the Gospel of Luke (see p. 7 above), the explanation is probably that when composing this v.51 Luke did not yet know that in Acts 1.4–9 he would later be able to use a much longer account. And it is also understandable that he did not simply want to omit this without any substitute.

[52] 'Return' is Lukan in language; 'great joy' takes up the same motif from v.41.

[53] The presence of the community in the temple is in accord with Lukan theology: the twelve-year-old Jesus already remains in the temple (Luke 2.46), as does the early community (Acts 2.46; 3.1; 5.42), which initially still understood itself as one Lukan group among many.

This last verse is a brief summary which has parallels in Luke-Acts (Luke 1.65f.,80; 2.20,40,51f.; Acts 1.14, etc.). In general, in any case we may attribute the last sentence to the evangelist, because here the author's intention is most to be expected and one may suppose that he kept the last word for himself.

Quite apart from the fact that the earliest Jerusalem community for many years still thought of itself as part of the Jewish temple community, no historical conclusions can be drawn from this section.

The Easter event according to Matthew

In his presentation of the Easter stories, in general Matthew bases himself on Mark's account and supplements this with two appearances of the Risen Lord (28.9f., to the women at the tomb; 28.16–20, to the eleven in Galilee), because the conclusion of Mark's Gospel (16.8) was as unsatisfactory for him as it was for Luke. Moreover he contributes a story about the guards at the tomb which provides a framework for the narrative of the journey of the women to the empty tomb, taken over from Mark, and depicts the opening of the tomb (vv.2–4).

The bribing of the guards at the tomb (Matt.27.62–66; 28.11–15)

62. Next day, that is, after the day of Preparation, the chief priests and the Pharisees gathered before Pilate
63. and said, 'Sir, we remember how that impostor said, while he was still alive, "After three days I will rise again."
64. Therefore order the sepulchre to be made secure until the third day, lest his disciples go and steal him away, and tell the people, "He has risen from the dead," and the last fraud will be worse than the first.'
65. Pilate said to them, 'You have a guard of soldiers; go, make it as secure as you can.'
66. so they went and made the sepulchre secure by sealing the stone and setting a guard.
. . .

11. While they [viz., the women] were going, behold, some of the guard went into the city and told the chief priests all that had taken place.

12. And when they had assembled with the elders and taken counsel, they gave a sum of money to the soldiers

13. and said, 'Tell people, "His disciples came by night and stole him away while we were asleep."

14. And if this comes to the governor's ears, we will satisfy him and keep you out of trouble.'

15. So they took the money and did as they were directed; and this story has been spread among the Jews to this day.

[62] The verse introduces the narrative with Matthaean vocabulary (e.g. 'gathered', 26.3,57; 27.17,27; 28.12). The note of time 'next day' follows from the 'evening' of v.57. In Matthew's time (c.85) the 'Pharisees' are the embodiment of the opponents of Jesus. For after the Jewish War (66–70), the conflict between Christians and official representatives of Judaism had become harsher. Strikingly, the session before Pilate takes place on the Sabbath (= Saturday), not for historical reasons but because this is necessary for the narrative. The death of Jesus on the Friday and the resurrection or discovery of the empty tomb two days after his death, the day after the Sabbath, were given by the Markan tradition (cf. Mark 16.1).

[63] The high priests and Pharisees explicitly 'remember' in their speech to Pilate a saying of Jesus that he would rise again after three days. This is obviously not a reference to the predictions of the passion, where Matthew (16.21; 17.23; 20.19), contrary to Mark, which he had before him (8.31; 9.31; 10.34), each time alters 'after three days' to 'on the third day' (cf. I Cor.15.4) but to Matt.12.40: 'For as Jonah was three days and three nights in the belly of the whale, so will the Son of man be three days and three nights in the heart of the earth.' In keeping with that, Pharisees are present in the scene in Matt.12.38–45, as they are here in Matt.27.62–66. The formula, which differs from the 'after three days' which Matthew uses elsewhere, is evidently meant to recall this passage.

If it is original (see 71ff., and esp. 84ff.), the Galilee tradition might be an important objection to the third day as the point of time of the resurrection. For if the resurrection took place in

Jerusalem on the third day, the first appearance of the risen Christ
cannot have taken place in Galilee that same day (cf. pp.52ff.). It
would have been too far for the disciples to travel from Jerusalem
to Galilee in that time. One possibility of avoiding this conclusion
would be to assume that the appearances took place in Galilee
and Jerusalem simultaneously, including the (first) appearance to
Mary Magdalene in Jerusalem on the third day.

Quite a different understanding arises from the following
observation: if one understands I Cor.15.4 ('that he rose on the
third day according to the scriptures') literally, only the resurrection of Jesus took place on the third day, and not the appearance
to Cephas, which remains undated (Luke 24.21 differs). This
suggests that the origin of the third day as a date should be sought
not in historical memories but in learned study of the Old
Testament.

Hosea 6.2 is the most likely point of reference for the phrase
'according to the scriptures' (I Cor.15.4). In the translation called
the Septuagint, the Greek version of the Old Testament, the
passage runs: Yahweh 'will make us whole after two days, on the
third day we will rise again and live before him'. This Hosea
passage was evidently used in Judaism to infer the date of the
resurrection of the dead at the end of the world. In that case the
resurrection of Jeuss will have been understood as the fulfilment
of an Old Testament prophecy.

One possible objection to a derivation of the third day from
Hos.6.2 is that this passage is not quoted anywhere in the New
Testament and that it appears in rabbinic scriptural exegesis only
at a relatively late date. However, one cannot conclude from the
fact that it was written down only at a later stage that it also arose
only later. On the contrary, I Cor.15.4 is possible evidence for a
Jewish eschatological interpretation of Hos.6.2.

[64] The verse contains Matthaean language: 'order' takes up
'ordered' (27.58); 'fraud' refers back to 'fraudster' in v.63. Verse
64c ('and the last fraud will be worse than the first') corresponds
to Matt.12.45c; 'the last state of that man becomes worse than
the first', i.e. if the disciples are left with their preaching of the
resurrection, then things will be even worse than they were with
Jesus.

[65f.] These verses tell how Pilate yields to the request of the
Jewish leaders.

Then follows Matt.28.1–10, the narrative of the empty tomb and the appearance of Jesus to two women disciples (see below 52ff.). Matthew next continues his account of the bribing of the guards at the tomb.

[28.11] 'While they (the women) were going' connects vv.10 and 11 in such a way as to suggest that vv.9f. and vv.11–15 took place at the same time. This link comes from Matthew, since the word used for 'go' is a favourite word of Matthew's and seems artificial here.

The (Roman) guards at the tomb themselves report to the Jewish leaders all that has happened, i.e. in fact about the resurrection of Jesus. So they know of this, just as it was clear to them that by his own testimony Jesus would rise after three days (27.63).

[12] The bribery of the guards recalls the bribery of Judas (26.15).

[13] This verse takes up 27.64. Although they know otherwise, the soldiers are to spread the rumour that the disciples stole the body while they themselves were sleeping. Precisely this had previously been the fear of the Jewish authorities. Now that Jesus has really risen, the soldiers are to start and spread the rumour of 'theft'.

[14] This provides the necessary supplement to the soldiers' action. Should the governor hear that the soldiers neglected their duty and slept on watch, the Jewish authorities will intervene with Pilate on their behalf.

[15] This verse concludes the story. The Roman soldiers do what the Jewish authorities ask of them. The second half of the verse looks forward to Matthew's time: 'and this story has been spread among the Jews to this day.'

The tale of the theft of Jesus' body by the disciples was evidently quite widespread among the Jews of Matthew's time. However, it cannot have been related in precisely this form, since here the Jews formally recognize the resurrection of Jesus. Like the crude negative portrayal of the Jews, this indicates an exclusively Christian shaping of the account.[44]

Hence the origin of the story can be conceived of as follows: Jews asserted that Jesus' body was stolen by the disciples. The Christians reacted to this with a story of the bribing of the guards at the tomb of the kind that we have in Matthew – unless we are to assume that Matthew composed the whole scene. These considerations can lead to the following historical judgments:

(a) No information can be established historically about the 'time of the resurrection'. The time 'on the third day' was chosen to fulfil an Old Testament prophecy (Hos.6.2).

(b) The rumour of the theft of the corpse of Jesus is certainly historical, but not the theft itself. For the disciples did not even know where Jesus had been 'buried', and furthermore, because of their utter disappointment, they would not have been in a position to perpetrate such a fraud.

(c) The tradition about the bribing of the guards cannot be taken seriously, because it too clearly has partisan features of Matthew or the Matthaean tradition. Moreover the guards would have been risking their necks in confessing that they had slept at the tomb.

The empty tomb and the appearance to the women (Matt.28.1–10)

1. Now after the sabbath, towards the dawn of the first day of the week, Mary Magdalene and the other Mary went to see the sepulchre.

2. And behold, there was a great earthquake; for an angel of the Lord descended from heaven and came and rolled back the stone, and sat upon it.

3. His appearance was like lightning, and his raiment white as snow.

4. And for fear of him the guards trembled and became like dead men.

5. But the angel said to the women, 'Do not be afraid; for I know that you seek Jesus who was crucified.

6. He is not here; for he has risen, as he said. Come, see the place where he lay.

7. Then go quickly and tell his disciples that he has risen from the dead, and behold, he is going before you to Galilee; there you will see him. Lo, I have told you.'

8. So they departed quickly from the tomb with fear and great joy, and ran to tell his disciples.

9. And behold, Jesus met them and said, 'Hail!' And they came up and took hold of his feet and worshipped him.

10. Then Jesus said to them, 'Do not be afraid; go and tell my brethren to go to Galilee, and there they will see me.'

[1] This verse can be explained completely on the basis of Mark. The reason why only two women come to the tomb in Matthew (who are identical with those of Matt.26.51), whereas there were still three in Mark, is that here Matthew probably felt a tension between Mark 15.47 and 16.1 and smoothed it out accordingly.

The women's intention in the Markan account, which is very striking – because it is unnecessary – , namely, to anoint the body in the tomb, and after three days at that, is absent from Matthew.

[2–4] There is a tension between vv.2–4 and vv.5–8, where again Mark's account is a basis: vv.2–4 describe the opening of the tomb by an angel from heaven, before whom the guards fall to the ground helpless; in vv.5–8 the message of the resurrection is addressed by the same angel to the women. The tremendous events in vv.2–4 have no relation to the delivery of the message in vv. 5–8. It may be conjectured that there is a tradition in vv.2–4 which was first put at this point by Matthew himself. By Matthew's insertion of vv.2–4 here, the women are indirectly made the witnesses to the very event of the resurrection.

The description of the opening of the tomb by an angel has a parallel in the Gospel of Peter (cf. v.17), of which a lengthy fragment was discovered in 1886 in the tomb of a Christian monk in Upper Egypt.

The fragment (the whole of it is written in the first person, Peter is the speaker) begins with a scene before Pilate. Then follows the request of Joseph of Arimathea for the body of Jesus, who in the Gospel of Peter is called only 'the Lord' (2.3–5), the mockery (3.6–9), the crucifixion (4.10), the inscription on the cross (4.11), the dividing of the garments (4.12), the intercession of the criminal crucified with the Lord (4.13f.), the darkness (5.15), the drinking of gall and vinegar (5.16), the last cry and death of the Lord (5.19), the rending of the veil of the temple (5.20), the deposition from the cross (6.21), the earthquake (6.21), the end of the darkness (6.22), the burial (6.23f.), the repentance of the Jews (7.25), the behaviour of Peter and the disciples (7.26f.), the setting of guards over the tomb (8.28–33), mass visits of the inhabitants of Jerusalem to the tomb (9.34), the resurrection (9.35–10.42), the report to Pilate and the command to the soldiers to keep silent (11.43–49), the women and the empty tomb (12.50–13.57), the return of the disciples to their homes

(14.58f.), Peter, Andrew and Levi go fishing (14.60). Here the fragment breaks off. On the basis of the parallels in the canonical Gospels one can conjecture with some justification that an appearance of the 'Lord' by Lake Tiberias followed (see below, 71ff.).

Here in the Gospel of Peter, after the opening of the tomb there is a description of the emergence of the revivified body of Jesus (9.35–11.43):

35. Now in the night in which the Lord's day dawned, when the soldiers, two by two in every watch, were keeping guard, there rang out a loud voice in heaven,

36. and they saw the heavens opened and two men come down from there in a great brightness and draw nigh to the sepulchre.

37. That stone which had been laid against the entrance to the sepulchre started of itself to roll and gave way to the side, and the sepulchre was opened, and both the young men entered in.

38. When now those soldiers saw this, they awakened the centurion and the elders – for they also were there to assist at the watch.

39. And whilst they were relating what they had seen, they saw again three men come out from the sepulchre, and two of them sustaining the other, and a cross following them,

40. and the heads of the two reaching to heaven, but that of him who was led of them by the hand overpassing the heavens.

. . .

43. Those men therefore took counsel with one another to go and report this to Pilate.[45]

A similar tradition also exists in the Ascension of Isaiah from the second half of the second century (= AscIs). In a summary account of the fate of Jesus (AscIs III.13–18) we read:

III.13. That he was to be crucified together with criminals, and that he would be buried in a sepulchre,

14. and that the twelve who were with him would be offended because of him, and the watch of the guards over the grave,

15. and the descent of the angel of the church which is in the heavens, whom he will summon in the last days;

16. and that the angel of the Holy Spirit and Michael, the chief of the holy angels, will open his grave on the third day,

17. and that the Beloved, sitting on their shoulders, will come forth and send out his twelve disciples,

18. and that they will teach to all the nations and every tongue the resurrection of the Beloved, and that those who believe on his cross will be saved, and in his ascension to the seventh heaven, whence he came.[46]

The existence of such descriptions of the resurrection raises the question whether these or similar narratives were unknown to Matthew. That can hardly be assumed. Rather, in the tradition which he used the angel evidently opened the tomb so that Jesus, restored to life again, could come forth. However, Matthew repressed this aspect and dispensed with a description of the resurrection of Jesus (but cf. Matt.27.51–53).

In both descriptions of the resurrection, as in the tradition presupposed in Matt.28.2, the dominant notion is that angels open Jesus' tomb on the third day and ascend into heaven with Jesus, who has been restored to life. There is much to be said for the view that the tradition was preserved at its purest in the Ascension of Isaiah and that the Gospels of Peter and Matthew belong more closely together. For only in them do the guards play an independent role; here already there is a development from the mere mention of them in the Ascension of Isaiah. However, the tradition in the Ascension of Isaiah is later than the tradition of the tomb in Mark, for here the notion of the resurrection is already fused with the legend of the empty tomb. – This presupposes (theological) reflection.

Thus we can note: *although in early Christianity alongside stories about the tomb and accounts of appearances the very event of the resurrection is depicted, these accounts of the resurrection are not an element of the earliest tradition or even 'eyewitness accounts', but late formations, which seek to satisfy the need for an explanation of how the resurrection of Jesus took place. So they have no historical value.*

Verses 5–8 again follow the account of Mark with a few deviations:

[5] This is parallel to Mark 16.6a.

[6] This corresponds to Mark 16.6b, where the statement of the resurrection is derived from a prediction of Jesus. This is absent from

Mark, who a little later (Mark 16.7) derives the future seeing of Jesus by the disciples from a prediction of Jesus.

[7] This has a parallel in Mark 16.7. However, the message is said to be directed only to the disciples as a whole; Peter is not mentioned by himself at all, as in Mark.

The content of the message of the angel has also shifted: in Mark it was that Jesus is going before the disciples into Galilee and they will see him there; here the content is the message of the resurrection of Jesus itself.

[8] In contrast to Mark (16.8: the women are silent for fear), this narrates that in fear (= taking up what is said in Mark) and in great joy the women want to pass on the message of the angel – they immediately believe. That is not surprising, since previously (vv.2–4) they have indirectly been made witnesses to the event of the resurrection. That is a good preparation for the next episode (vv.9–10), in which Jesus will appear directly to them.

[9–10] These verses have no parallel in Mark. They depict an encounter of Jesus with the two women mentioned in v.1, who take hold of his feet (cf. II Kings 4.27) and worship him (cf. later v.17).[47] Jesus orders them not to fear, and to tell his brothers (cf. Matt.18.15f., and esp. 23.8: 'you have one teacher, and you are all brethren') to go to Galilee, where they will see him.

There is much to be said for supposing that these verses do not go back to pre-Matthaean traditions. For apart from his greeting, the risen Jesus does not say anything to the women at the tomb other than what the angel has already told them in v.7. So this is mere repetition. However, it should be noted that here we have 'brothers' rather than 'disciples' (vv.7f.): in particular, this expresses the close connection between Jesus and his disciples who together have gone through the despair of suffering and death. With the resurrection they are finally appointed 'brothers of Jesus'. There are no distinctions of rank among them, nor is Peter mentioned separately in Matt.28.7 – he no longer has any preferential status. However, the disciples have a pupil-teacher relationship with Jesus (Matt.23.8–10) – despite their brotherly relationship to one another.

A far simpler question arises in connection with vv.9 and 10 – if the verses come from Matthew himself. Why has he written the same thing twice at such a close interval? Thus another possibility for the origin of Matt.28.9–10 seems more illuminating. Despite the Matthaean expressions, the verses are fundamentally to be regarded as an independent passage which is not connected to the tomb of Jesus at all. This is endorsed by the fact that C.H.Dodd established that Matt.28.9–10, Matt.18.16–20 and John 20.19–21 have a parallel structure.[48] The situation presupposed in each case is that the followers of Jesus have been deprived of their Lord. Then follows his appearance (Matt.28.9,17; John 20.19), a greeting (Matt.28,9; John 20.19), recognition by the disciples (Matt.28.9,17; John 20.20) and a commission (Matt.28.10,19; John 20.21f.). This suggests that Matthew has used a piece of already existing tradition.

It also means that in the material which Matthew used in Matt.28.9–10, there need not necessarily have been women; there may have been the disciples or another group. It was Matthew who first put together all the 'parts' (vv.1,2–4,5–8,9–10) at his disposal in order to create a better transition between the story of the tomb and the concluding appearance of Christ. In that case, for him the only possible recipients of the vision were the women, who on the basis of the previous narrative were the only ones to have been present (cf. Matt.26.56; 27.55,61). So Matthew would have replaced the 'disciples' who originally belonged in these verses with the 'women'.

The reason for shaping the scene in this particular form will have been so as to 'connect with the empty tomb not only an encounter with an angel but also an encounter with the risen Christ'.[49] This development leading up to the accounts of the appearance of the risen Christ became a general tendency; confronted with the questions of outsiders and on the basis of personal reflections, the story of the tomb and the accounts of the resurrection had to be brought increasingly close together. In John 20.1–18 this later led to a scene depicted in a broad and vivid way, whereas in Luke's world (around a decade earlier, see p.7 above), only the appearance of an angel seems to have gone with the tradition of the empty tomb, and no real narrative of an appearance (this is attested by Luke 24.22–24).

Be this as it may, at least on the basis of Matt.28.9f., the tradition of an appearance to women (or to Mary Magadelene) at the tomb of Jesus proves to be unhistorical. We shall see below whether this verdict also applies to John 20.14–18.

Matt.28.16–20: The appearance of Jesus and the mission command

At this point Matthew reports a further appearance of Jesus which is similar to that in 28.9f. (cf. above, pp.56f.).

16. Now the eleven disciples went to Galilee, to the mountain to which Jesus had directed them.
17. And when they saw him they worshipped him; but some doubted.
18. And Jesus came and said to them, 'All authority in heaven and on earth has been given to me.
19. Go therefore and make disciples of all nations, baptizing them in the name of the Father and of the Son and of the Holy Spirit, teaching them to observe all that I have commanded you; and lo, I am with you always, to the close of the age.'

Generally speaking, it is striking that the account of Jesus' appearance is so brief. It is expressed only by a meagre 'when they saw him'; here the reaction of the eleven disciples is identical to that of the women in Matt.28.9 (they worshipped him). The centre of the scene here is not the appearance itself, but the subsequent words of Jesus (vv.18–20).

[16] This describes the carrying out of Jesus' command from v.10. The 'mountain' here is a preferred place for appearances (cf. 5.1; 15.29; 17.1). Matthew himself shaped the verse as an introduction to what follows.

[17] 'They worshipped him' takes up the same verb from v.9. 'Doubt' appears in the New Testament elsewhere only in Matt.14.31, and along with the 'fall down' which is often used by Matthew (2.2; 4.9; 8.2, etc.) may similarly come from him.

The motif of doubt (cf. especially below, 69ff.) addresses problems of Christians of the second and third generation, who no longer have any direct access to the original Easter experience and who – like us today – had difficulty in imagining it. They recognize their own situation in the text and are more inclined to accept Jesus' answer to this question which is oppressing them.

[18] 'Came' is typically Matthaean language (4.3; 8.19; 9.28, etc.). There are numerous parallels in the redactional material to 'he spoke to them and said' (cf. only 13.3; 14.27; 23.1). In v.18b the notion of the appointment of the Son of Man as ruler (cf. Dan.7.14)

is transferred to Jesus. With the exception of Matt.9.6 (= Mark 2.10), the phrase 'in heaven as on earth' occurs as a whole or in part only in Matthew, and not in Mark (6.10; 16.19; 18.18).

[19] 'Go' takes up 'they went' (v.16). For this favourite term of Matthew's cf. 9.13; 10.7; 18.21; 21.6, etc. Other words in this verse certainly come from Matthew himself, thus 'therefore' (3.8; 6.8f.; 6.31, 34, etc.) and 'make disciples' (13.52; 27.57).

The 'nations' probably refers only to the Gentiles. Matthew is still too much in the Jewish tradition to be able to include the Jews in the term 'nations', which is reserved for the Gentiles. His sharp polemic (ch.23) applies to the Judaism newly constituted by the Pharisees, which in this form no longer belongs among the nations.

[20] This verse is full of Matthaean expressions: 'observe', 'all', 'command', 'and behold' (cf.28.9), 'end of the world'.

In this final section of his Gospel Matthew is answering the question of the basis of the Easter certainty and the overcoming of doubt. He points to the exclusive authority of the sayings of Jesus for the present. The preaching has become the preaching of the commandments of the Torah, the Jewish law, rightly understood. The earlier Easter appearances have now been replaced in the Matthaean community by the words of the exalted Christ present in preaching and in the Gospel. Here, in vv.18–20, Matthew uses a tradition available to him. Three elements are visible:

1. Verse 18b: the exaltation of Jesus and the power bestowed on him with it (cf. Matt.11.27; John 3.35; Phil.2.9–11).

2. Verses 19–20a: the mission charge. Presumably Matthew has replaced a command 'preach the gospel', which was perhaps preserved in the secondary conclusion to Mark (16.15), in the text that he had before him, with the invitation 'make disciples' (cf.13.52; 27.57). The triadic formulation of baptism 'in the name of the Father and of the Son and of the Holy Spirit' is striking, since in the early period baptism was simply in Christ (Gal.3.27) or in the name of Jesus (I Cor.1.13; Acts 8.16; 19.5; cf. Did.9.5).[50] Probably this was a baptismal formula with a liturgical character which has a parallel in Didache 7.1 (a church order from the beginning of the second century). This runs, 'Baptize in the name of the Father and of the Son and of the Holy Spirit.'

3. Verse 20b: Jesus' promise of his everlasting presence to the end of the world (cf. Matt.18.20).

It is almost impossible to decide whether these three elements were originally independent and were brought together by Matthew at this point, or whether Matthew had already found them combined as a unit.

In this connection the following point must also be made: there is really no longer an appearance tradition in vv.18–20, although with his meagre 'when they saw him' Matthew is indicating that here he wants to relate an Easter story. Rather, what we find here is Easter theology, which forces any story of an appearance to the side or replaces it with words of the risen Christ. In this way the scene remains open to the present. So what we have is almost no longer an appearance but an enthronement of Jesus as Lord of heaven and earth, which here, as often, is directly connected with the resurrection, indeed is even identified with it. Perhaps it would therefore be better to term the event an appearance of the enthroned Christ.

So the motif of authority as such does not serve to distinguish the risen Christ from the earthly Christ, but rather combines the two. What is new is the universal extension of the authority of the risen and the earthly Christ over heaven and earth. The special feature of the text is therefore not just the combination of appearance and mission, but that of exaltation and mission to the nations.

The historical yield is extremely limited. Matthew and/or his tradition concentrate later theological conclusions like the 'mission to the nations' in the closing scene. These conclusions were never drawn in this form by the disciples themselves, but by Paul and Jewish Hellenistic Christians. Nevertheless, it must be said quite emphatically that these conclusions were already implicitly contained in the experience of the resurrection (religious language always means more than it says).

It is pertinent that Jesus appeared (to Peter and) to the twelve[51] (I Cor.15.5), in other words that they saw him and on the basis of this experience formed a community which preached the resurrection and exaltation of Jesus as the Messiah and/or the Son of Man among their Jewish contemporaries. That is the historical nucleus of the scene reported by Matthew. Whether this vision took place in Galilee, as the text indicates, remains uncertain on the basis of the present passage, since Matthew has inferred 'Galilee' from Mark 16.7. But on the basis of general considerations (see 71ff. and especially 84ff.), the location of this first 'vision' in Galilee may be historically correct.

The Easter event according to John

John contains the greatest number of Easter stories in comparison with the Gospels of Matthew, Mark and Luke (the Synoptic Gospels). That may simply be because the Gospel was composed at a later period when a larger number of traditions were generally known than in the early period. However, at the same time this indicates a problem: if the traditions underwent a long development, it becomes incomparably more difficult to work out the original traditions and their historical background.

The visit of the disciples to the tomb and the appearance to Mary (John 20.1–18)

1. Now on the first day of the week Mary Magdalene came to the tomb early, while it was still dark, and saw that the stone had been taken away from the tomb.
2. So she ran, and went to Simon Peter and the other disciple, the one whom Jesus loved, and said to them, 'They have taken the Lord out of the tomb, and we do not know where they have laid him.'
3. Peter then came out with the other disciple, and they went toward the tomb.
4. They both ran, but the other disciple outran Peter and reached the tomb first;
5. and stooping to look in, he saw the linen cloths lying there, but he did not go in.
6. Then Simon Peter came, following him, and went into the tomb; he saw the linen cloths lying,
7. and the napkin, which had been on his head, not lying with the linen cloths but rolled up in place by itself.
8. Then the other disciple, who reached the tomb first, also went in, and he saw and believed;
9. for as yet they did not know the scripture, that he must rise again from the dead.
10. Then the disciples went back to their homes.
11. But Mary stood weeping outside the tomb, and as she wept she stooped to look into the tomb;

12. and she saw two angels in white, sitting where the body of Jesus had lain, one at the head and one at the feet.

13. They said to her, 'Woman, why are you weeping?' She said to them, 'Because they have taken away my Lord, and I do not know where they have laid him.'

14. Saying this, she turned round and saw Jesus standing, but she did not know that it was Jesus.

15. Jesus said to her, 'Woman, why are you weeping? Whom do you seek?' Supposing him to be the gardener, she said to him, 'Sir, if you have carried him away, tell me where you have laid him, and I will take him away.'

16. Jesus said to her, 'Mary.' She turned and said to him in Hebrew, 'Rabboni!' (which means Teacher).

17. Jesus said to her, 'Do not hold me, for I have not yet ascended to the Father; but go to my brethren and say to them, I am ascending to my Father and your Father, to my God and your God.'

18. Mary Magdalene went and said to the disciples, 'I have seen the Lord'; and she told them that he had said these things to her.

A. John 20.1–2

[1] This corresponds to Mark 15.2,4a. The question 'Who will roll away the stone for us from the tomb?' (Mark 16.3) can be omitted, because the purpose of the visit (the anointing of Jesus' corpse) is not given here. However, the construction in v.1b has great similarity to the parallel Luke 24.1f. As in Matt.28.1f., Mary Magdalene is mentioned as subject. In all the Synoptics, in contrast to John, several women go to the tomb (Mark 16.1, three; Matt.28.1, two; Luke 24.1, more than three; cf. Luke 8.2f. and Luke 24.10). Mary Magdalene's early visit to the tomb is an expression of her love, which may be the reason for her visit anyway. The body of Jesus has already been buried (John 19.40), so that she does not need to worry about it.

[2] This verse depicts how Mary rushes to Peter – evidently without first looking into the tomb. The verse sets off the following, new interlude, the race between Peter and the Beloved Disciple to the tomb, which is developed in vv.3–10. The plural 'we do not know' does not necessarily require several women to have been to the tomb (cf. John 3.2; 14.5). But possibly the plural does reflect

several women, since in v.13 (cf. v.15) the singular appears when Mary Magdalene's lament is repeated word for word.

B. John 20.3–10

This section has a close parallel in Luke 24.12 (see pp.34ff. above) and in Luke 24.24. It is a narrative the main motive of which is 'beyond doubt the rivalry of the two disciples and, connected with that, the emphasis on the Beloved Disciple'.[52] The 'other disciple' mentioned in v.3 could be identical with him.

Already in John 13.23–25; 18.15–16; 19.26–27,35, the author of this Gospel inserts into the passion narrative this person who is to be a witness guaranteeing its authenticity. At the same time the figure represents the ideal disciple of Jesus. In comparison to the generally recognized position of Peter, the Beloved Disciple embodies the proximity of the Johannine community to Jesus; i.e. the other disciple becomes an unassailable authority (cf. John 14.6f.). Here the rivalry between the Johannine community and other Christian communities is evidently reflected in the race of the two disciples to the tomb. The other disciple sees the cloths first (v.5), and v.8 explicitly says that he believed (in contrast to Peter!).

However, this is in tension with v.8; according to this verse he still must have been as uncomprehending as Peter. Therefore v.9 is either a later addition, or the verse originally belonged to the tradition which said that Peter (and his companion) did not believe (cf. Luke 24.12: Peter wonders at what had happened). In that case John himself would have inserted v.8 without completely removing the tension with v.9.

Because of his love (or the love of Jesus for him), this other disciple hastens more urgently than Peter, just as because of this he also stayed by the cross to the last (cf. John 19.26). In v.7 the rolled-up cloths are evidence of the impossibility of a tomb-robbing, since this would have been done in great haste, and the linen cloths would hardly have been folded up carefully. The author of the Fourth Gospel is opposing Jewish slander in a different way from the legend of the guards at the tomb (Matt.27.62–66; 28.11–15). Thus in the Johannine understanding the empty tomb almost becomes a testimony in itself to the resurrection of Jesus.

As both disciples still do not understand, they can simply go home as though nothing had happened (v.10). No more is said about their discovery, because of the section after next, vv.19–23, in which Jesus makes a surprise appearance among all the assembled disciples. Only there do they come to understand properly.

The section vv.3–10 goes back to a tradition which contains an account of a visit of Peter to the tomb (he so to speak repeats the experience of the women for Mark 16.1–8, which has a parallel in Luke 24.12). This piece of tradition is the foundation for the composition of the race between Peter and the beloved disciple by the author of the Gospel of John.

C. John 20.11–18

[11] This verse picks up the broken threads of v.2. The join is rough. According to v.2 Mary is not standing at the tomb at all, and the two disciples play no role for her. Now suddenly 'in vv.11ff. she is standing at the tomb as though the events recounted in vv.3–10 had not happened'.[53] 'She stooped to look' (into the tomb) takes up 'stooped to look' from v.5. Mary Magdalene mourns Jesus (cf. John 16.20) and weeps.[54] She has not yet gained the knowledge of the 'other' disciple.

[12] This has a parallel in Mark 16.5. In the present text the motifs of the angel and the tomb have been lavishly elaborated. That there are two angels corresponds to Luke 24.4, so there could be a connection between the two texts.

[13]: 'They have taken away my Lord' picks up the same phrase from v.2.

[14] For the incomprehension of Mary Magdalene cf. Luke 24.16: 'But their eyes were kept from recognizing him'; John 21.4: 'The disciples did not know that it was Jesus.'

[15] The address by Jesus to Mary Magdalene, 'Woman, why are you weeping?', is identical word for word with the address of the two angels to Mary Magdalene in v.13. Mary's reply is shaped by a misunderstanding (cf. John 7.35; 8.22, but see the preliminary ignorance of Peter [13.7] and the disciples [John 16.18]), but also shows her love for Jesus, for whom she still wants to care in death.

[16] 'She turned round' picks up the same verb from v.14. The verse depicts the recognition scene (cf. Luke 24.30f.), which is

introduced by the mention of Mary's name. Mary's reaction ('Teacher') surpasses the address 'Sir', from v.15, which was addressed to the 'gardener'. The term occurs elsewhere in the New Testament only in Mark 10.51, and is synonymous with the address 'Rabbi', which occurs in the Gospel of John with reference to Jesus more frequently than in the other Gospels.

[17] 'Do not hold me, for I have not yet ascended to the Father', indicates that Mary is still subject to a possible misunderstanding. The command can be understood in different ways.

1. No contact has taken place, nor is it to take place (perhaps because the Lord has not yet ascended to the Father and contact could prevent him from doing this).

2. Contact takes place, but is to be ended (perhaps because Jesus has not yet attained real heavenly corporeality).

3. The words have a transferred meaning and the question of contact or non-contact is open, to the degree that the Risen Christ can be touched at all (cf. the faith of the other disciple in John 20.8).

One can also combine one or more of these possibilities with a symbolic understanding, as e.g. Johannes Lindblom does. He translates: 'Do not cling to me, for I am not yet ascended to the Father, but I am in process of ascending to him . . .'[55] Mary's effort to cling to Jesus then stands as a symbol for the anxiety of the disciples about having to part from Jesus.

The way in which the recipients of the message are addressed as 'my brethren' is striking. The expression 'my brethren' appears in the same context of an instruction of the Risen Lord in Matt.28.10 and probably denotes members of the Christian community (cf. Matt.18.15; I John 2.9–11, etc.; III John 3). At any rate, such a use is unique in the Gospel of John, apart from 21.23.

The content of the charge in v.17c, which certainly derives from John himself, has a parallel in John 16.28b: 'I am leaving the world and going to the Father' (cf. 16.5,10, etc.). But now the talk is no longer only of the Father of Jesus but also of the Father of the disciples, of Jesus' God who is also their God. The author means to say that through the departure of Jesus his Father becomes the Father of his followers. 'The real Easter faith therefore is that which believes this; it consists in understanding the offence of the cross.'[56]

[18] This verse narrates the execution of Jesus' command to Mary Magdalene; she tells the disciples (as Jesus' brethren), 'I have seen the Lord', which does not really fit Jesus' command. As the statement

sounds like a formula and corresponds to I Cor.9.1 ('Have I not seen Jesus our Lord?'), John wants it if possible to give Mary Magdalene emphatic legitimation as a witness to the resurrection.

The tradition used here by John was originally an appearance story, which John first linked with the story of the tomb known from Mark, and into which he inserted vv.3–10. Whether here John was using the Markan report directly or used a related tradition or a tradition influenced by Mark 16.1–8 makes no difference here. In so doing John may have reduced the two women given by the tomb tradition to one: Jesus appears to Mary Magdalene. However, she only recognizes him when he has addressed her by her own name, just as the Emmaus disciples first recognize Jesus by his gesture in the breaking of the bread.

The narrative has a Johannine form throughout (cf. v.17 and the parallel between the address to Mary in v.16 and John 10.3). However, the nucleus may go back to the independent tradition of an appearance of Jesus to Mary Magdalene, the wording of which we can no longer reconstruct. The (Hebrew!) form of address 'Rabboni' used to Jesus may indicate an early Palestinian origin here, even if it is unclear whether this is attached to the tradition of an appearance of Jesus to Mary Magdalene. The artistic form of the resurrection narrative suggests that it was elaborated like this only at a later date, that is, if this form is not John's own work. But who would dispute that at least an essential part of the message of Jesus is contained, or has been preserved, in the nucleus of these words?

It seems historically certain that Mary Magdalene was witness to an appearance of the risen Jesus. However, the question remains whether the historical conclusion that Mary was the first to see the risen Jesus can be drawn from the fact of an independent tradition of this appearance.

Now Mary Magdalene was certainly a follower of Jesus, indeed he had healed her of seven evil spirits (Luke 8.2). In later tradition from the time of Gregory the Great (around 600), Mary Magdalene is identified with Mary of Bethany (Luke 10.38–42: John 11.2f.; 12.3, etc) and the woman who was a sinner in Luke 7.36–50, thus connecting her demon-possession with her former life of vice. Unfortunately this attractive identification is pure speculation and so no account of it will be taken in what follows. *Furthermore, we can conclude from her name 'Magdalene' (= from Magdala, a place on the western shore of Lake Gennesaret in Galilee), and the way in which her person is attached to the passion narrative, that she took part in the fateful journey to Jerusalem along with Jesus and others. Nevertheless, the tradition of an appearance of Jesus to Mary Magdalene is evidently fairly late.*

The risen Christ appears to the disciples (John 20.19–23)

19. On the evening of that day, the first day of the week, the doors being shut where the disciples were, for fear of the Jews, Jesus came and stood among them and said to them, 'Peace be with you.'
20. When he had said this, he showed them his hands and his side. Then the disciples were glad when they saw the Lord.
21. Jesus said to them again, 'Peace be with you. As the Father has sent me, even so I send you.'
22. And when he had said this, he breathed on them, and said to them, 'Receive the Holy Spirit.
23. If you forgive the sins of any, they are forgiven; if you retain the sins of any, they are retained.'

[19] The note of time takes up that in v.1. Whereas there it was early in the morning, now it is the evening of the same day (Sunday). Otherwise there is no connection with the previous narrative. There is no reference either to the message of Mary (v.13) or to the scene with the disciples at the empty tomb (vv.3–10). That suggests a basis in tradition for the present scene, for John himself would have made a smoother transition.

'For fear of the Jews'[57] appears similarly word for word in John 7.13; 19.38; cf. 9.22. In the parallel narrative Luke 24.36–43 the fear in v.37 is a reaction to the appearance. This seems to have been the original place for the 'motif of fear'. There the formula 'he stood among them' (v.36), which comes from Luke, corresponds almost word for word with the phrase used in the present verse. One explanation could be the use of the Gospel of Luke by John, especially as the formula 'in the midst' is unusual for John.

The appended greeting, 'and he said to them, "Peace be with you"', similarly goes back to Luke because of the word-for-word correspondence with Luke 24.36b.

[20] The demonstrative showing of his hands and his side (= taking up John 19.34) is remarkable at first glance, is done for no recognizable reason, and is probably governed by Luke 24.40. Perhaps this is meant to emphasize further 'that the Risen Lord and the Crucified are one'.[58] Furthermore the verse prepares for the next scene (vv.24–29), in so far as the disciples do not need to touch Jesus to believe, but Thomas will demand to do so (see below, 69ff.).

Verse 20b depicts the reaction of the disciples ('that they saw the Lord' corresponds to 'I have seen the Lord' [v.18]). The motif of the joy of the disciples recalls Luke 24.41. The parallel can again be explained from a literary relationship.

[21] The further greeting comes from John. This repeats the greeting from v.19 and touches on the mission of the disciples (cf. John 17.18). However, the fact that the saying about mission has been *formed* by John does not mean 'that the motif of the sending of the disciples by Jesus was first introduced by the evangelist as such into the report in his source,'[59] since Gal.1.15f. in particular suggests that a type of appearance account followed by an mission charge from Jesus is relatively old. There Paul derives his mission charge directly from his vision of the risen Christ ('he revealed his Son to me, in order that I might preach him among the Gentiles'). However, the linguistic form of the charge can no longer be reconstructed.

[22] There are parallels in the Old Testament and elsewhere to the receiving of the spirit by being breathed on (Gen.2.7; Ezek.37.5–10,14; Wisdom 15.1). However, this is highly untypical of John: for him Jesus *is* at the same time the personified Spirit (cf. John 14.16; 16.7,13; cf.7.39). So his formulation is surprising at this point. Moreover the absence of an article in the phrase 'receive Holy Spirit' is unique – a phrase which occurs only here in the Gospel of John, but has a parallel in Acts 2.4.

[23] The idea of the 'forgiveness of sins' is elsewhere unknown to the Fourth Evangelist and so like the previous verse may derive from tradition. The closest parallels to the authority spoken of in this verse are Matt.16.17f.; 18.18 and Luke 24.46 (this passage has been used here).

In general it may be said that the tradition used here presupposes Luke 24.36–49. The material which may be presumed to underlie it contained an undated report about a sudden appearance of Jesus among his disciples. The disciples were terrified. Jesus invited them (perhaps as a reaction to their doubt) to touch him and gave them the Spirit with an archaic gesture of breathing on them, sent them (into the world?) and at the same time promised them authority to forgive sins.

Simply because of the dependence on the Lukan account we can rule out the possibility that the traditions come from an eye-witness report. Nevertheless, it seems old and in parts 'authentic'. That applies to the combination of 'seeing' and 'being sent', and 'seeing' and 'being filled' with Holy Spirit. This event, which can also be recognized in the 'original' account by Paul, forms the historical nucleus of the tradition of John 20.19–23. Would it be going too far to see here (together with Luke 24.36–43) a reflection of the appearance to the Twelve?

However, the fleshly objectification of Jesus is a secondary addition and unhistorical (v.20). The original seeing of the Easter witnesses was a seeing in the spirit; they did not see a revived corpse.

Doubting Thomas (John 20.24–29)

The narrative has no parallel among the Easter stories. Thomas is not known elsewhere as an Easter witness and his stubbornness is also unique (cf. v.25b).

24. Now Thomas, one of the twelve, called the Twin, was not with them when Jesus came.
25. So the other disciples told him, 'We have seen the Lord.' But he said to them, 'Unless I see in his hands the print of the nails, and place my finger in the mark of the nails, and place my hand in his side, I will not believe.'
26. Eight days later, his disciples were again in the house, and Thomas was with them. The doors were shut, but Jesus came and stood among them, and said, 'Peace be with you.'
27. Then he said to Thomas, 'Put your finger here, and see my hands; and put out your hand, and place it in my side; do not be faithless, but believing.'
28. Thomas answered him, 'My Lord and my God!'
29. Jesus said to him, 'Have you believed because you have seen me? Blessed are those who have not seen and yet believe.'

The present story is in tension with the previous story, since according to vv.21–23 all the disciples except Judas, and this must have included Thomas as one of the Twelve, were given the authority to forgive sins.

[24] This verse explains why the appearance to Thomas happens or had to happen: he was not there when the coming of Jesus just described (vv.19–23) took place. Outside the four lists of the disciples (Mark 3.18; Matt.10.3; Luke 6.15; Acts 1.13), Thomas appears in the New Testament only in the Gospel of John (11.16; 14.5; 20.24; 21.2). He appears here as a typical representative of doubt (cf. Matt.28.17; Mark 16.11,13,14; Luke 24.11,25,38,41).

[25] 'We have seen' takes up '(they) saw' from v.20 and 'I saw' from v.18. The second part of the verse depicts a crass materialism as the condition of Thomas' faith. The demand to put a hand into Jesus' side refers back to John 19.34a. The use of nails in the crucifixion of Jesus appears elsewhere only in the Gospel of Peter 6.21 and probably goes back to the Greek translation of Ps.21.17, which reads 'They pierced my hands and my feet'.

[26] The note of time 'after eight days' puts the further meeting of the disciples, like the first, on a Sunday. Verse 26b repeats v.19b word for word. Jesus comes to his disciples, although the doors are shut, and greets them.

[27] This verse takes up v.2 and corresponds exactly to Thomas' wish from vv.25f. For touching as a means of being convinced of the reality of the body of Jesus and the identity of his personality cf. Luke 24.39–43. However, the appended invitation ('and do not be faithless, but believing') indicates what really counts.

[28] Thomas does not accept Jesus' offer. He exclaims 'My Lord and my God' (cf. John 10.30), and with that confession comes to believe. He is used to address the readers, who are to see here, as in the confessions of Simon (John 6.68f.) or Martha (John 11.27), a model for their own faith. There is no longer any need for touching, since the word of Jesus alone creates faith.

[29] This verse also speaks in a reproachful tone only of a seeing (and not of a touching) by Thomas and has the general form of a beatitude (in the Gospel of John elsewhere only in John 13.17): what matters is not seeing but faith. That is not far removed from Matt.28.16–20, where 'the message of the Risen One and obedience to his word was the way to the overcoming of doubt'.[60]

The reproach to Thomas evidently applies to all the other

disciples, since Thomas has not asked for any other proof than what Jesus has voluntarily offered the others. Thus 'the doubt of Thomas is representative of the common attitude of those who cannot believe without seeing miracles (4.48)'.[61]

The Thomas story represents a late stage of the early Christian Easter stories. It does not have a close relationship to the original Easter events. Apparently it is meant to counter the Gnostic conviction that Jesus was 'only' a divine being – not a human being – in a phantom body without flesh and blood (cf. similar tendencies in the Johannine epistles: I John 1.1; 43.1f.; II John 7 and also Luke 24.39–43). This assertion is refuted by Jesus' 'manifest' offer to let himself be touched.

Because of its reference back to John 20.19–23, we should most probably see the narrative as John's own creation, used to make concrete and illustrate the widespread motif of doubt. This is also suggested by the similarity in the structure of the Thomas story to John 1.45–51,[62] and the fact that individuals are often given a special role in the Gospel of John (Nicodemus [John 3.1–9], Mary and Martha [John 11.1ff.], Philip and Nathanael [John 1.43–51], the woman of Sychar [John 4.7ff.]). Therefore we can follow Anton Dauer in drawing this conclusion:

'The evangelist has attached to the figure of Thomas the theme of the unbelief of the disciples, its overcoming through an encounter with the risen Lord and the treatment of the problematical question of the value of such faith.'[63] Here he transfers the motif of doubt which he evidently removed from John 20.9–23 to the present story. This incident involving the Risen Jesus and Thomas is unhistorical.

The risen Christ by the Sea of Tiberias (John 21)

1. After this Jesus revealed himself again to the disciples by the Sea of Tiberias; and he revealed himself in this way.
2. Simon Peter, Thomas called the Twin, Nathanael of Cana in Galilee, the sons of Zebedee, and two others of his disciples were together.
3. Simon Peter said to them, 'I am going fishing.' They said to him, 'We will go with you.' They went out and got into the boat; but that night they caught nothing.

4. Just as day was breaking, Jesus stood on the beach; yet the disciples did not know that it was Jesus.

5. Jesus said to them, 'Children, have you any fish?' They answered him, 'No'.

6. He said to them, 'Cast the net on the right side of the boat, and you will find some.' So they cast it, and now they were not able to haul it in, for the quantity of fish.

7. That disciple whom Jesus loved said to Peter, 'It is the Lord.' When Simon Peter heard that it was the Lord, he put on his clothes, for he was stripped for work, and sprang into the sea.

8. But the other disciples came in the boat, dragging the net full of fish, for they were not far off from the land, but about a hundred yards off.

9. When they got out on land, they saw a charcoal fire there, with fish lying on it, and bread.

10. Jesus said to them, 'Bring some of the fish that you have just caught.'

11. So Simon Peter went aboard and hauled the net ashore, full of large fish, a hundred and fifty-three of them; and although there were so many, the net was not torn.

12. Jesus said to them, 'Come and have breakfast.' Now none of the disciples dared to ask him, 'Who are you?' They knew it was the Lord.

13. Jesus came and took the bread and gave it to them, and so with the fish.

14. This was now the third time that Jesus was revealed to the disciples after he was raised from the dead.

15. When they had finished breakfast, Jesus said to Simon Peter, 'Simon, son of John, do you love me more than these?' he said to him, 'Yes, Lord, you know that I love you.' He said to him, 'Feed my lambs.'

16. A second time he said to him, 'Simon, son of John, do you love me?' He said to him, 'Yes, Lord, you know that I love you.' He said to him, 'Tend my sheep.'

17. He said to him the third time, 'Simon, son of John, do you love me?' Peter was grieved because he said to him the third time, 'Do you love me?', and he said to him, 'Lord, you know everything; you know that I love you.' Jesus said to him, 'Feed my sheep.

18. Truly, truly, I say to you, when you were young, you girded yourself and walked where you would; but when you are old, you will stretch out your hands, and another will gird you and carry you where you do not wish to go.'

19. This he said to show by what death he was to glorify God. And after this he said to him, 'Follow me.'

20. Peter turned and saw following them the disciple whom Jesus loved, who had lain close to his breast at the supper and had said, 'Lord, who is it that is going to betray you?'

21. When Peter saw him, he said to Jesus, 'Lord, what about this man?'

22. Jesus said to him, 'If it is my will that he remain until I come, what is that to you? Follow me!'

23. The saying spread abroad among the brethren that this disciple was not to die; yet Jesus did not say to him that he was not to die, but, 'If it is my will that he remain until I come, what is that to you?'

24. This is the disciple who is bearing witness to these things, and who has written these things; and we know that his testimony is true.

25. But there are also many other things which Jesus did; were every one of them to be written, I suppose that the world itself could not contain the books that would be written.

This chapter has clearly been attached to John 20 at a subsequent stage, as emerges for the following reasons:

1. 20.30f. is explicitly the conclusion to a book.

2. 21.24f. introduces the Beloved Disciple as the author of the whole Gospel, while there are no references whatsoever to this author in chs.1–20.

3. John 21 sometimes has different language from John 1–20. Cf. especially 'children' (v.5) as an address to the disciples and 'brothers' (v.23) as a designation of the Christians.[64]

However, this finding does not amount to any preliminary decision about the age of the traditions contained in John 21. Still, we are now to regard as the author the one who composed John 21 as an addition. He is not necessarily identical with the author of John 1–20.

A. *The appearance of Jesus by the Sea of Tiberias (John 21.1– 14)*

[1] This verse corresponds to v.14 and comes from the author of this chapter ('he revealed himself' [twice] in v.1 prepares for 'was revealed' in v.14). In both verses John 20 is presupposed. 'For the third time' (v.14) describes the appearance narrated in John 21.2– 13 as the third. In that case 20.19–23 would be the first and 20.26–29 the second appearance to the disciples. The appearance to Mary Magdalene (20.11–18) is evidently not counted, as it was not an appearance to disciples.

[2] This begins with a list of the persons involved: 'Simon Peter' refers back to 20.2, 'Thomas who is called the twin' to 20.24. For Nathanael cf. John 1.45–49. The additional mention of the sons of Zebedee may go back to earlier tradition, as they are not mentioned elsewhere in the Gospel of John. By contrast the two disciples who are not described further because of the reference back in 'his disciples' to v.1 are not part of the tradition. All in all, this produces the number seven, which has symbolic value. It stands for the future church (cf. also the seven churches in Rev.2–3).

[3] This is the condensed narrative of an unsuccessful fishing trip. There is a parallel in Luke 5.5, 'We have toiled the whole night and caught nothing.' Here it is striking how the six disciples are subordinated or attached to Peter: Peter makes the decision, the disciples follow.

[4] The note of time, 'as day was breaking', follows on from 'that night' in v.3. The story of a failed fishing trip becomes the story of an appearance of Jesus. Like Mary Magdalene before them (John 20.14), the disciples do not recognize Jesus (cf. Luke 24.16). There is no longer any differentiation between Peter and the disciples.

Verses 2–4a belong to the tradition of a fishing trip which, as Luke 5 shows, was connected with an account of the calling of Peter (see 84ff. below).

[5] The familiar form of address 'children' appears elsewhere only in I John 2.14,18. The Greek word for 'food' can also be translated 'fish'. The author is already thinking here of the meal described later, and is concerned that first the fish shall be caught (v.6) which are needed for the meal (cf. Luke 24.41f.).

[6] This contains Jesus' command to the disciples to cast the net. They obey him and 'were not able to haul it in, for the quantity of fish' (cf. Luke 5.4–6). The failure noted at the end of v.5 becomes an abundant success because of Jesus' instructions and the way in which they are obeyed.

[7] This is an interlude inserted by the author, involving the Beloved Disciple and Peter. As in John 20.8, it is emphasized that the Beloved Disciple recognizes Jesus *before* Peter. So he surpasses him a second time (thus also in 21.20–23). When Peter learns that it is the Lord, after putting on his upper garment he immediately throws himself into the sea to swim to Jesus. This action expresses his great love for him (v.15).

[8] This is about the other disciples and explains why Peter could leap into the water (and swim to Jesus); he was only about 100 yards off shore.

[9] This brings together the catch of fish and the (Lord's) meal.

[10] This reports that fish from the abundant catch are to be part of the meal, although there were already fish on the fire (v.9). 'This discrepancy is best explained on the assumption that the author of the chapter wants to combine the story of the catching of the fish and the account of an appearance (which included the meal).'[65]

[11] Peter again takes a central role in the story. He is the one who (now!) alone drags the net and the 153 fish to shore. This emphatic information about the number of the fish and the fact that the net did not break on the one hand stresses the miraculous character of the event (cf. John 6.13) and on the other calls for further interpretation. Perhaps for the author the event is a symbol for the church and the large number of fish expresses its openness to all the world. Here – as in Matt.16 – Peter again seems to be the guarantor of this church.

[12] The first part of the verse with Jesus' invitation to breakfast does not fit well with the second. What has the statement that no one dared to ask Jesus who he was to do with Jesus' invitation to a meal? According to the next clause they even knew that he was the Lord. There is a remarkable tension here between the disciples' desire to ask and their alleged knowledge. It was caused by the author of the chapter – because of the Beloved Disciple, who in fact had already recognized Jesus in v.7.

[13] The introduction of the sentence with 'Jesus came'

corresponds to the beginning of 20.18 ('Mary Magdalene came'). The gesture of dividing the bread and the fish recalls John 6.11. At any rate the gestures of Jesus explain that the Risen Lord is present (cf. Luke 24.30). The disciples now no longer need to ask the question for which according to v.12 they did not have the courage.

Verses 12–13 come from the tradition of an Easter appearance which originally also included v.4b.

[13] See above on v.1.

It may be regarded as historically certain that Peter (and the disciples) had an experience after Jesus' death in which Jesus appeared to him/them as the Risen Christ. The tradition about catching the fish in vv.2–4, which has a parallel in Luke 5 (there, however, it takes place in the lifetime of Jesus), may recall this appearance. We shall have to look at it more closely in connection with the appearance to Peter (see below, 84ff.).

The tradition behind the meal of the risen Jesus with his disciples is relatively late. The Lord's Supper is understood as a symbol of encounter with the risen Lord. Thus the presence of this tradition merely confirms that an appearance of Jesus to the disciples took place in some form: however, the link with a 'supper' is to be regarded as unhistorical.

B. *The Risen Christ and Simon Peter (John 21.15–19)*

[15–17] The section vv.15–19, a conversation between Jesus and Peter, has an integrated structure. Jesus asks Peter three times whether he loves him. 'More than the others' in the first question (v.15) serves as a link to the previous unit, which mentions disciples. Each time Peter answers in the affirmative. Before the last answer it is reported that Peter was grieved because Peter had asked him a third time – apparently the first answers had not been enough. The reaction to Peter's answer is on each occasion followed by a command of Jesus to his disciple: v.15 end, v.16 end, v.17 end. This structure is artificial. The Greek verb of the first and third commands is identical ('feed my lambs/sheep'), as is the object ('sheep') in the second and third requests: the question generally is Peter's position of leadership in the church. Is it chance that Peter is to do what according to John 10 Jesus himself does, namely to be the good shepherd? At all events, a deliberate literary shaping of the text by the author emerges from the careful construction.

[18–19] These verses report a further dialogue in which Jesus predicts Peter's crucifixion. Here the disciple is being singled out in a special way (see also v.19, 'glorify God'). Then in conclusion follows the invitation 'Follow me'; i.e. the third command, 'Feed my sheep' (v.17), is supplemented by the invitation to personal discipleship of Jesus, which (because of vv.18–19a) is a call to martyrdom. Here there is a manifest reference to John 13.36, and it is said that only now is it possible for Peter to become a disciple of Jesus, since despite his denial he has received forgiveness of sins. In other words, Peter is rehabilitated.

The last observation shows how the author wanted the scene to be understood. The denial of Jesus by Peter has been 'overcome' by the repeated commissioning of Peter. Here the threefold structure of the dialogue is perhaps an imitation of the denial of Jesus by Peter, which is also narrated three times in the Gospel of John (John 18.17, 25–27).

It is sometimes inferred from this that there is no old tradition in the present narrative. But can it be ruled out that the author of ch.21 dropped a connection in the tradition between the commissioning and the denial? It is possible that the present text is a remnant of the connection between the denial and the experience of grace as originally reported, all the more so since this is also probable in the basic material common to Luke 5 and John 21.1–13. However, it has to be conceded that such a thesis cannot be developed from an isolated consideration of the text. We shall be concerned with this later (88f.), when we look specially at the historicity of the denial of Jesus by Peter.

At all events, the tradition underlying John 21.15–17 also derives from the recollection of a first appearance of Jesus to Peter from the earliest post-Easter period. An appearance of Jesus to Peter is certainly historical. Peter interpreted this appearance as a commission from Jesus to preside over the community (cf. Matt.16.18, below 86ff.).

C. Peter and the disciple whom Jesus loved (John 21.20–23)

The section once again (after John 20.3ff.; 21.7) illuminates the relationship between Peter and the Beloved Disciple.

[20] Since it is said that the Beloved Disciple is (already) following Jesus, while Peter only receives the invitation in v.19, the Beloved Disciple is once again given a spiritual superiority. The verse consciously refers back to the scene at the Last Supper (John 18.15).

[21–22] Since Jesus had prophesied the crucifixion of Peter in v.18, Peter asks him about the destiny of the Beloved Disciple. The author of chapter 21 picks up a saying current in his community that the Beloved Disciple would not die before the return of Jesus and seeks to explain its real meaning. For that, he uses a conversation between Jesus and Peter. Jesus tells Peter that it is no concern of his whether the Beloved Disciple remains alive until he himself comes again. Rather, Peter is to follow him (= an endorsement of the call to discipleship in v.19 and the preeminence of the Beloved Disciple over Peter).

[23] This verse corrects the expectation of the members of the community (= brethren) that the Beloved Disciple will not die before the return of Christ and explains this assumption as a misunderstanding. Jesus did not prophesy this, but only presented it as a possibility.

The fact that a false expectation about the survival of the Beloved Disciple had to be corrected is meant to remove all doubt about the historical existence of this disciple.

The conversation in vv.20–23 between Peter and Jesus is meant to clarify two points:[66]

(a) Peter's authority has passed on to the Beloved Disciple (Peter has to die a martyr's death, while the Beloved Disciple remains).

(b) Despite his death the Beloved Disciple remains the guarantor of the Johannine community, since in v.24 he is regarded as the author of the Gospel of John.

This should have made it clear that the whole section derives in its entirety from the imagination of the author of ch.21. Earlier traditions have not been used; there is no historical background.

Results of the analysis of the accounts of Easter

1. All four Gospels of the New Testament report in extended descriptions a visit of women followers or disciples of Jesus to the

tomb of their Master. This visit is said to have taken place on the third day after the crucifixion. They find it empty, and each time they are given the news that Jesus has been raised. In three of the Gospels the risen Jesus meets them a short time later and gives them specific instructions.

1. The narratives of the visits to the tomb have been formed around Mary from the town of Magdala in Galilee; the persons going with her to the tomb are interchangeable. Thus the historicity of the event stands or falls with the credibility of Mary's visit to the tomb. Mary was certainly a follower of Jesus and went with him to Jerusalem. She is a fixed element of the passion tradition (see above, 26ff.). But her visit to the tomb of Jesus is not historical: the source of the tradition is a legend which came into being at a late stage, directed against attacks by opponents, and this presupposes an already extant 'Christian' belief in the resurrection of Jesus (see 61ff. above, where Peter's visit to the tomb was also shown up to be unhistorical).

2. The date of the resurrection 'on the third day' cannot be substantiated historically. The point in time was conjectured because it fulfilled an Old Testament prophecy (Hos.6.2, see above 49f.).

3. The investigation of the burial of Jesus already suggested that his followers did not even know where their leader had been buried (see above, 22f.). The analysis of the story of the guards at the tomb (Matt.27.62–66; 28.11–15), which apparently demonstrates that the place of Jesus' burial was very well known both to the authorities and to the disciples (for how otherwise could the tomb have been guarded?), proves to be a legend developed only later, to counter the rumour of a theft of Jesus' corpse which was in fact going the rounds (see above, 57ff.).

4. The actual event of the resurrection of Jesus is not described in any text of the New Testament. However, there are detailed statements about it outside the biblical writings. But these are all products of the imagination, which seek to answer the question of the manner of the resurrection of Jesus (see above 56ff.).

5. Soon after his crucifixion Jesus appeared to some persons. But the earliest appearance did not take place at the tomb, since the tradition of the tomb and the tradition of Jesus' appearance did not originally belong together. Only in the subsequent period were they brought increasingly close together, so that the manner of the original appearance became almost unrecognizable.

Here in general we are to assign a relatively late date of origin to those reports which emphasize the corporeality of the risen Christ, although elements in them could be much later. For the emphasis on a reality of the risen Jesus which could be perceived with the senses developed only later, in order to make it possible to maintain the reality of the resurrection over against other assertions that Jesus was not raised at all, but was only a spirit or a phantom.

6. It may be taken as historically certain that Peter and the disciples had experiences after Jesus' death in which Jesus appeared to them as the risen Christ.

7. Both Jerusalem (and its environs) and Galilee are mentioned as scenes of these events. However, had the first appearances taken place in Jerusalem, it would be impossible to explain those in Galilee. For why should the disciples have gone back to Galilee *after* their resurrection appearance? After all, the earliest community came into being in Jerusalem, the centre of Jewish faith.

For the same reason it is also difficult to imagine how anyone could have invented Galilee as the place in which Jesus appeared. That leaves only the conclusion that the first appearance in fact took place in Galilee and subsequent ones in Jerusalem, but only at a later date. This conjecture is supported by the fact that the appearance in John 21 takes place by Lake Tiberias (i.e. in Galilee), and the mention of this place comes from an early tradition (see above, 71ff. and especially below, 84ff.).

8. But that makes it impossible for these appearances already to have happened on the third day after the crucifixion. The disciples could not have returned from Jerusalem to Galilee in this period, from Friday to Sunday. Moreover the sabbath intervened, when they could hardly have travelled. But at the same time we should note that in the earliest mention in I Cor.15.4, only the resurrection of Jesus and not his appearance is dated to the third day.

9. The Gospels mention a first appearance to Mary Magdalene, which is firmly bound up with Jerusalem. It seems to be historically certain that Mary Magdalene experienced an appearance of the risen Jesus. Either this appearance took place later, namely when the news of appearances of Jesus had reached Jerusalem from Galilee, or Jesus appeared simultaneously in several places. In that case it would in fact be impossible to decide who had had the earlier appearance – Peter or Mary. But the

tradition of a first appearance to Mary arose relatively late (see above, 64ff.), whereas that to Peter is among the earliest pieces of tradition. This is a good reason for regarding the *first* appearance to Mary as unhistorical.

10. Also bound up closely with the environs of Jerusalem (Emmaus) is the appearance of Jesus to two disciples, one of whom is called Cleopas. Individual features of this are certainly old. It may be conjectured that Cleopas was a cousin of Jesus. This relationship would also explain why an independent tradition formed over this appearance. For in antiquity family relationships were held to be particularly important: a blood relationship to lofty figures was understood virtually as a status symbol (see below 101f.). Thus slowly reports and legends formed around these people. So we may conjecture that appearances of the risen Jesus to members of his family in fact took place, but we are in the dark as to precisely when.

11. Finally, reference should be made to the appearance to Thomas, which was shaped by the evangelist John himself, and thus is to be taken to be unhistorical (see above, 69ff.).

None of the stories that we have investigated comes from eye-witnesses; they have passed through the hand of the community and/or a theologically trained figure. So the historical yield on the resurrection of Jesus is thus far unsatisfactory. So far we know only that an event of the kind that the Gospels suggest is historically improbable. The accounts of the resurrection of Jesus and its accompanying circumstances are all to be understood as attempts to explain the inexplicable: this has nothing to do with the real historical event. So the enterprise of reconstructing the resurrection event seems to have got into a cul de sac.

The only thing that we can certainly say to be historical is that there were resurrection appearances in Galilee (and in Jerusalem) soon after Jesus' death. These appearances cannot be denied. But did the risen Jesus in fact reveal himself in them? If this can be demonstrated, then for the future we can happily dispense with the question how the resurrection took place. For in that case the establishment of the fact of the resurrection would be quite enough to reinforce our Christian faith.

So we shall now look closely at the resurrection appearances known to us from I Cor.15.

The appearances of the risen Jesus

In investigating the resurrection appearances we shall limit ourselves
to the 'seeings' mentioned by Paul in I Cor.15. The reason for this is
that the investigations of the additional appearances (to Mary and
Cleopas) have not given us any indication of the manner of the seeing
over and above the fact of the seeing. All the elaborations have been
seen to be unhistorical. So it is impossible to enquire further behind
these appearances.

The situation with the phenomena mentioned by Paul looks
different. For what is said about the resurrection appearance to Paul
himself is an eye-witness report. Moreover Paul expressly regards
Jesus' appearance to himself as identical to the appearances to other
witnesses (I Cor.15.8). Evidently no one doubted this, either, for
despite some opposition Paul was recognized as a full witness to the
resurrection.

In enumerating the appearances of the risen Christ in I
Cor.15.5–8, in the original Greek text Paul always uses a form of the
verb 'see'. However, a straight translation causes difficulties.

This term has a prehistory in the Old Testament. The Greek
version of the Old Testament (= Septuagint) uses it wherever a
corresponding Hebrew term is used in connection with the appearance of Yahweh or his angel to Abraham (Gen.12.7; 17.1; 8.1), Isaac
(Gen.26.2, 24), Jacob (Gen.31.13; Gen.35.1,9), Moses (Ex.3.2).
This happens around forty-five times. In view of this frequent usage,
scholars have spoken of a 'theophany formula' which recurs in the
creed I Cor.15 and have drawn far-reaching consequences from it.
But if it is used merely as a formula, then the word itself ('see,
appear') does not say more than an actual origin through 'seeing'. In
that case it denotes only an 'appearance' of some kind.

However, it has to be pointed out that in the Septuagint the
expression can also have other subjects than God: II Kings 14.11
(Joash and Amaziah); I Macc.4.6 (Judas); I Macc.4.19 (Judas'
enemies); I Macc.9.27 (a prophet); II Macc.3.25 (a horse). Here we
may speak of a well-worn or unspecific use of the word. So the matter
is not as simple as all that.

In I Cor.15 Paul uses the verb form for a variety of phenomena
(individual encounters, mass manifestations). Elsewhere, too, the
appearances cannot have been of the same kind. For Cephas, the
experience of the 'appearing' is first of all a direct event. It was not

preceded by any process of communication (no one told him that Jesus was risen and had appeared) or even a consolidation of the community (as with other members in the chain of witnesses). He had an independent, isolated experience.

The latter is also true of Paul. But the difference between Peter and Paul is that Peter saw Jesus again, whereas Paul had not known Jesus beforehand. The appearance of Christ to Paul similarly became a real first experience, because it affected someone who had persecuted the community and was not a believing member.

Since on the other hand Paul uses 'he appeared' with reference to himself (v.8) and thus puts his encounter with Jesus in parallel with the appearance of Jesus to the other witnesses, and since moreover in other passages he uses different verbs to express his seeing of the risen Christ, it is legitimate to attempt to clarify the phenomenon mentioned in I Cor.15 by these passages. The analysis of the Pauline texts will therefore play a key role later.

The first appearance to Peter

In the first period of the earliest community in Jerusalem Peter had been its leader. This may already be concluded from Gal.1.18: Paul travelled to Jerusalem three years after his conversion to get to know *Peter*. How Peter attained this position can most plausibly be explained as the result of a legitimation by 'the risen Christ'. I Corinthians 15.5 refers to this resurrection appearance, which may be said to be historical, as does the old 'Easter cry of joy' in Luke 24.34 ('The Lord has risen indeed and has appeared to Simon'). There is also a reaction to the first appearance outside the New Testament, in a text which has already been discussed, Ignatius, To the Smyrnaeans 3.1–2 (see 45f. above).

However, it is strange how little the texts report of this first appearance to Peter, which was so important for the founding of the first Christian community. The reason for this may be that Peter had declined very rapidly in importance in the earliest community. For in the controversy over the question whether the strict Jewish law still has any significance for Christians, the main part of the earliest community which was more faithful to the law, under the leadership of James, won the day over the Peter party, which was freer of the law. This shook Peter's reputation. He finally left

Jerusalem, went on a missionary journey, and died under Nero in Rome (c.65).

In view of this development in early Jerusalem Christianity, we can understand why traditions about Peter gradually became weaker and were displaced by narratives about James. It is not at all surprising that at the time when the Gospels were composed, Peter's initial role as leader of the earliest Jerusalem community was mentioned only peripherally. But that does not mean that he was never leader!

Nevertheless, scanty remnants indicating that Peter originally saw Christ have been preserved in the New Testament, namely in Luke 5.1–11/John 21 and Matt.16.17–19.

Luke 5.1–11/John 21

The story about the 'fishers of men' in Luke 5.1–11 takes place in the lifetime of Jesus. So here his resurrection is not mentioned as such:

1. While the people pressed upon him to hear the word of God, he was standing by the lake of Gennesaret.
2. And he saw two boats by the lake; but the fishermen had gone out of them and were washing their nets.
3. Getting into one of the boats, which was Simon's, he asked him to put out a little from the land. And he sat down and taught the people from the boat.
4. And when he had ceased speaking, he said to Simon, 'Put out into the deep and let down your nets for a catch.'
5. And Simon answered, 'Master, we toiled all night and took nothing! But at your word I will let down the nets.'
6. And when they had done this, they enclosed a great shoal of fish; and as their nets were breaking,
7. they beckoned their partners in the other boat to come and help them. And they came and filled both the boats so that they began to sink.
8. But when Simon Peter saw it, he fell down at Jesus' knees, saying, 'Depart from me, for I am a sinful man, O Lord.'
9. For he was astonished, and all that were with him, at the catch of fish which they had taken;
10. and so also were James and John, sons of Zebedee, who

were partners with Simon. And Jesus said to Simon, 'Do not be afraid; henceforth you will be catching men.'

11. And when they had brought their boats to land, they left everything and followed him.

In the introductory comments, (above 7ff.) it was said that the evangelists put the individual actions of Jesus in a quite arbitrary chronological order. So we must keep asking whether a narrative is correctly placed where it appears.

Usually one can only speculate on such a question, since there is no basis for a clear answer. But in this special case the narrative John 21.1–17 can be of some help. It contains interesting parallels to the Lukan story (cf. above, 71ff.), which arouse the suspicion that the two narratives belong together and originally go back to a resurrection story.[67] There are the following parallel motifs:

1. Peter as the main character in the narrative (after Jesus);
2. the unsuccessful fishing trip;
3. the allusions to Peter's denial (the confession of sins in Luke 5.8b and the threefold question of Jesus in John 21.15–17);
4. the abundant catch (John 21.6/Luke 5.6);
5. the motif of catching, each time in connection with Peter (Luke 5.10/ John 21.11);
6. the summons to discipleship (Luke 5.11/ John 21.19);
7. the honouring of Peter by a saying of the Lord (Luke 5.10c/ John 21.17d).

In particular we note that John 21.15–17 in its present form does not represent an old tradition of the link between denial and experience of pardon. So the third and sixth points listed above are not an original part of the story. But on the basis of the other parallels cited it remains very probable that on the basis of John 21 the narrative Luke 5.1–11 can be called a former Easter story, all the more so since the Lukan version of the saying about catching men (Luke 5.10) addressed to Peter urgently requires the saying to be rooted in the Easter situation.[68]

In a similar situation the earlier Markan text 1.16–18 reports only the promise of a future appointment to be fishers of men:

16. And passing along by the Sea of Galilee, he saw Simon and Andrew the brother of Simon casting a net in the sea; for they were fishermen.

17. And Jesus said to them, 'Follow me and I will make you become fishers of men.'
18. And immediately they left their nets and followed him.

By contrast, Luke 5.10 depicts the appointment itself, which follows immediately with this saying addressed to Peter. Furthermore, Mark 1.18 contains a summons to discipleship which has been adapted to the circumstances of Jesus' life only at a secondary stage, whereas Luke 5.10 has the call 'Fear not!'. This has hardly developed from Mark 1.18, but originally already stood in the story of the appearance. It fits Easter perturbation in the face of encounter with the risen Christ.

Another important indication of a fundamental resurrection situation is that Luke 5.8b narrates 'a desperate confession of guilt on the part of Peter, for which there is no occasion in the situation presupposed in Luke 5'.[69] Should Peter's denial of Jesus be deemed historical (see below, 92f.), then provisionally the significance of the historical event underlying Luke 5 can be described as 'being forgiven profound guilt and being appointed a witness and apostle of the living Lord'.[70]

Of course not every revelation scene is automatically to be rooted in the Easter event. But here this origin is very probable.

So Luke 5/John 21 go back to the tradition of an appearance of the risen Jesus; of course we are not well informed about its details, especially as both texts have been formulated from a later perspective.

Matthew 16.15–19

There is probably a further report of the first appearance of Jesus to Peter, again formulated from a later perspective, in Matt.16.15–19.

15. He said to them, 'But who do you say that I am?'
16. Simon Peter replied, 'You are Christ, the Son of the living God.'
17. And Jesus answered him, 'Blessed are you, Simon Bar-Jonah! For flesh and blood has not revealed this to you, but my Father who is in heaven.
18. And I tell you, you are Peter, and on this rock I will build my church, and the powers of death shall not prevail against it.

19. I will give you the keys of the kingdom of heaven, and whatever you bind on earth shall be bound in heaven, and whatever you loose on earth shall be loosed in heaven.'

Rudolf Bultmann already defended, with good arguments, the considerable antiquity of this passage.[71] He wrote: 'The community handed down a saying of Jesus in which Peter is promised authority in matters of doctrine or discipline' (38). That follows, he argued, from the verbs 'loose' and 'bind' in v.19. The whole idea of v.18 points to earliest times: 'The words can hardly have been formulated in any other place than in the earliest Palestinian community, where Peter was looked up to as the founder and leader of the community and the blessing of Peter was put into the mouth of the risen Lord. For it is doubtless the risen Lord who speaks in Matt.16.17–19 . . .' (258).

In that case the original ending of the story of Peter's confession, which Mark already reports in Mark 8.27–30, would appear in Matt.16.17–19. Mark would have rejected this ending and replaced it by the discussion between Jesus and Peter (Mark 8.3–33) which culminates in Jesus' rejection of Peter's view with the words 'Get behind me, Satan' (v.33b). This would now be 'polemic against the Jewish-Christian view represented by Peter from the standpoint of the Hellenistic Christianity of the Pauline sphere' (258, cf. Mark 8.32f.).

Bultmann's important conclusion from his reflections is: 'If the supposition be correct, that Matt.16.17–19 is the original conclusion to the confession scene, it also indicates that the Easter experience of Peter was the hour when the messianic faith of the earliest community was born. In that case the whole narrative would have to be designated an Easter story which was carried back into the life of Jesus (perhaps first by Mark)' (258f.)

It is probable that at first stories of Peter's Easter experience were in circulation in the community. These laid claim to being the first appearance. But above all because of the changing power relationships and the situation of rivalry in the earliest Jerusalem community, these traditions were soon distorted and put in other narrative contexts. Nevertheless, the historical verdict may be expressed that *Peter heard and saw Jesus alive after his death*. With this 'seeing' was connected the task of mission and leadership of the church and the granting of authority to forgive sins. How far the last three points were the historical object of the appearance or arose subsequently from Peter's interpretation is difficult to say with any certainty.

Now one could break off the historical investigation with these remarks and regard any further investigation as historically impossible, especially as the situation with the sources is so bad. Here the commandment of historical reason not to speculate where the sources give out indeed applies. On the other hand, the Peter traditions of the New Testament may not have been completely exhausted in respect of the Easter appearance to Peter. That applies in particular to the tradition of a denial of Jesus by Peter, which is said to have taken place at the very point of Jesus' arrest. In all probability Luke 5.8 already referred to this tradition. Should it be historical, it seems likely that the denial of Jesus (before his death) and the seeing of Jesus (after his death) should be connected; this might possibly provide a deeper access to the resurrection appearance to Peter.

The denial of Jesus by Peter (Mark 14.54,66–72)[72]

After his arrest, Jesus was taken before the high priest:

> 54. And Peter had followed him at a distance, right into the courtyard of the high priest; and he was sitting with the guards, and warming himself at the fire.
>
> . . .
>
> 66b. One of the maids of the high priest came;
> 67. and seeing Peter warming himself, she looked at him, and said, 'You also were with the Nazarene, Jesus.'
> 68. But he denied it, saying, 'I neither know nor understand what you mean.' And he went out into the gateway.
> 69. And the maid saw him, and began again to say to the bystanders, 'This man is one of them.'
> 70. But again he denied it. And after a little while again the bystanders said to Peter, 'Certainly you are one of them, for you are a Galilean.'
> 71. But he began to invoke a curse on himself and to swear, 'I do not know this man of whom you speak.'
> 72. And immediately the cock crowed a second time. And Peter remembered how Jesus had said to him, 'Before the cock crows

twice, you will deny me three times.' And he broke down and wept.

The whole narrative refers back to the prediction of the denial in Mark 14.30, which is identical in wording with v.72c.

[54] The beginning of the narrative has been put there by Mark in order to link the narrative to the account of the hearing before the Supreme Council (vv.53, 55–65). Verse 66a ('as Peter was below in the courtyard') takes up the thread broken off in v.43. 'Warming himself' (v.67) refers back to 'warming' in v.54.

The interlocking of the two events produces an impressive contrast between Jesus' confession before the Supreme Council (Mark 14.62) and Peter's denial.

For Mark, the significance of the link between the denial and the hearing before the Supreme Council is doubtless a contrast between Jesus' confession (Mark 14.62) and Peter's threefold, i.e. total, denial. This blatant contrast warns Christians to follow the example of Jesus in public confession.

Mark has also intervened within the narrative itself: traces of Markan linkage or typically Markan terminology appear in the picking up of 'high priest' (v.66 refers to v.53) and 'warming himself' (v. 67 picks up v.54). 'With the Nazarene'[73] (v.67), 'again', 'began' (v.69); 'again', 'and immediately' (v.70); 'he remembered' and 'the word'[74] (v.72) come from Mark. Possibly Mark wrote the whole of v.72, which refers to 14.30.

[66–68a] These verses portray the first denial. Strictly speaking this is a denial by Peter that he is a disciple (cf. v.67b) and not yet a denial of Jesus. But since Peter's reply in v.68a at the same time rejects any knowledge of Jesus, the concrete denial of Jesus in v.71 is prepared for. Here the text achieves a cumulative effect: the questions to Peter become more intense and more oppressive, so that he can no longer resort to general remarks about not understanding, but has to become concrete.

[68b–70a] These portray the second denial, which takes place in the courtyard. In contrast to the first, it is not described in detail, but only mentioned briefly. In keeping with this the maid merely 'informs' the bystanders about Peter (and no longer addresses him, as on the first occasion). The cumulative effect is achieved by the increase in the number of people involved in the scene who press Peter with the question whether he belongs to the Jesus circle. This question from the bystanders to Peter is not actually described, but presupposed, as Peter refers to it ('but again he denied it'). 'Again' picks up the same word from v.69 and is used again in v.70, probably to emphasize the chain reaction of question and denial.

[70b–71] These relate the third denial. The setting is apparently the same as for the second denial (the forecourt), but this is not explicitly mentioned. This time the bystanders take the initiative. The maid had already told them who Peter was in the second denial scene. Thus the second and third denial scenes are closely related. The assertion of the bystanders is supported by the fact that Peter (like Jesus) is a Galilean. First they confirm what the maid has just (v.69b) told them, and this time they address Peter directly. This third denial of Peter is most strongly emphasized by cursing and swearing. Only now is there a concrete denial of Jesus. In this way 14.30 (the announcement of the denial) is first really fulfilled.

[72] This verse closely links the denial in Mark 14.54f., 66–71 with its announcement in Mark 14.27–31, after the event. Just as Jesus in Mark can look towards the coming denial of Peter, so earlier he has known in advance about the betrayal by Judas (Mark 14.8– 21) and his own death and resurrection (Mark 8.31; 9.31; 10.32–34).

The question disputed by scholars whether at this point Mark has extended what was originally narrated as a single denial to a threefold denial can be left aside here. It can hardly be decided with sufficient certainty, and is unimportant for the question of the historicity of the denial, which is what concerns us. At all events it is certain that the tradition of the denial once circulated in an isolated form independently of the passion narrative, as the link between the two only took place at a later stage, and that there was a tradition – albeit one which cannot be marked out with any certainty – of a denial of Jesus by Peter. *This might have a historical nucleus, since it is inconceivable that the community would have invented such a humiliating legend about its leader.*

Before making a new proposal about the origin of this tradition, we must first examine the relationship of the tradition of the denial to a tradition which deviates from it. This appears in Luke 22.31–34.

The relationship between Mark 14.66–72 and Luke 22.31–34

31. 'Simon, Simon, behold, Satan demanded to have you, that he might sift you like wheat,
32. but I have prayed for you that your faith may not fail; and when you have turned again, strengthen your brethren.'
33. And he said to him, 'Lord, I am ready to go with you to prison and to death.'
34. He said, 'I tell you, Peter, the cock will not crow this day, until you three times deny that you know me.'

Rudolf Bultmann already pointed out that there is a great difficulty in these brief verses. For 'Verses 33f. look out of place after vv.31f., since v.32 ended with a forward look to Peter's great role, whereas vv.33f. contain only the tragic obverse of that.'[75] So it is hardly possible that all these verses originally belonged together.

It has therefore been conjectured that the passage has been constructed wholly by Luke, i.e. has no nucleus of tradiiton. But this raises a new difficulty. Can we imagine that a writer like Luke, who is so concerned for inner harmony, did not notice striking contradictions in successive sentences?

By contrast, Bultmann's theory, which attributes Luke 22.31 to tradition and concludes that Luke himself formulated 22.32–33, is more illuminating. The piece of tradition in Luke 22.31f. is, Bultmann continues, important above all for two reasons: '1. It shows that some elements of the passion narrative also had a separate tradition. 2. Verses 31, 32a evidently presuppose that in the "sifting" of the disciples all but Peter have fallen away; only his loyalty has not wavered. So this tradition does not know the story of the denial' (267). The image of the sifting of the wheat presupposes that not all the disciples have fallen away, but that a remnant has survived the 'sifting'; and the statement of Jesus 'that your faith does not waver' virtually excludes any falling away on Peter's part (267 n.1).

Thus it has become clear that the tradition of Luke 22.31f. which speaks of an apostasy of the disciples and a persistence of Peter in the face of Jesus' passion, and the tradition of a denial of Jesus by Peter, are in tension. One could conclude from this that the denial is unhistorical. But it is equally conceivable that the tradition in Luke 22.31f. sought to correct an existing tradition of the denial and therefore put particular emphasis on the steadfastness of Peter. Moreover it would be conceivable that the tradition – despite the denial – wanted to affirm in retrospect 'that Peter in no way completely abandoned the cause of Jesus . . . but was in some way concerned to keep faith with it'.[76]

The denial of Jesus by Peter – a historical fact

Günter Klein argues that the denial of Peter is unhistorical. He gives a biographical interpretation of its threefold repetition and associates it with the turning points in Peter's career: first he was a member of the circle of the Twelve, then he was an apostle, after that a member of the college of the pillars and finally a lone figure.[77] But who could have interpreted this as *betrayal*? Moreover, where can we locate the opposition of Peter from which the anti-Petrine tradition of the denial would have to be derived?

By contrast, it is better to revive the old proposal of Martin Dibelius that Peter himself told of his denial, 'though not in connection with his description of the passion so much as in connection with his Easter experience'.[78]

Over and above this one can point as a parallel to the way in which Paul's past and his present preaching of the gospel was reported. In Gal.1.23 it is said: 'They had only heard: he who once persecuted us is now preaching the faith he once tried to destroy.' This verse is an oral tradition which circulated in the churches of Syria persecuted by Paul and which may similarly have been known in the church which he had founded. Indeed Paul explicitly refers in the context of Galatians to the fact that the Galatians had heard of his activity as a persecutor (Gal.1.13).

Similarly, the denial of Peter and his Easter experience were reported in a 'once-now' scheme. In both cases we evidently have personal traditions with a high content of historical truth.

Peter had distanced himself from his master in Jerusalem after Jesus' arrest in order to save his life. In this he was like his fellow disciples, who had already taken flight previously (Mark 14.50). The historicity of the flight of the disciples is certain. The disciples of Jesus must have left him – otherwise they themselves would have been crucified.

Another disciple, Judas, had even co-operated in Jesus' arrest. Presumably there were considerable tensions in the group of disciples around Jesus after the decisive journey to Jerusalem. There were formal rifts. The saying about Satan in Mark 8.33 (see above, 87f.) is too sharp not to be authentic, and indicates tensions in the relationship between Jesus and his 'first disciples'. There was a catastrophe, and the togetherness was abruptly ended by the execution of Jesus.

Peter's Easter experience – a process of mourning

I shall now attempt on the basis of the story of Peter and the fact of his vision of the Risen Jesus to depict what may have happened within him between Good Friday and Easter.

For Peter, in the drama of the situation of Good Friday and his denials, the world had collapsed. At Easter the word of Jesus, i.e. the word of Jesus' forgiveness, once again came to Peter, mourning as he was, despite his denial of Jesus and despite Jesus' death; he 'saw' Jesus. That Peter's situation can be described as one of mourning is evident from a comparison with reports by mourners, which ocasionally also contain the element of the image of the presence of a beloved person who has died.

Yorick Spiegel[79] cites some cases:

> The mourner hears the step of the dead person on the stair, hears the gravel crunch in front of the house and believes that the door is opening: 'I saw Kay standing inside the house door. He looked as he always did when he came back from work. He smiled, and I ran into his outstretched arms as I always used to do and leaned against his breast. I opened my eyes and the image had disappeared' (171).

Moreover, in addition to hallucinations and auditions there is almost more frequently the feeling that the dead person is present:

> 'I still have the feeling that he is near, and that there is something that I should do for him or tell him . . . He is always with me. I hear him and see him, although I know that he is only an idea . . . .' (173).

In conjunction with his descriptions, Spiegel explains that a gradual parting from the dead person is part of successful mourning. This parting takes place as the real person gradually fades away and takes a long time, differing in extent from individual to individual.

From this perspective, however, Peter's mourning of the dead Jesus would not be successful but unsuccessful mourning. For Peter does not gradually take his farewell, nor does he let the real appearance of Jesus fade away step by step. Rather, he breaks off the mourning process abruptly by replacing the dead Jesus with a living picture of Jesus which is true to reality. The psychological explanation of this fact could be that Peter wanted to make Jesus unconditionally alive again, because he could not bear his mourning. *Here we come up against a problem that we shall encounter later in discussing Paul's conversion.*

Now the question arises whether this interpretation does justice to events. To explain this we must look at further publications on the topic of mourning.

Research into cases of mourning and the painful loss associated with them carried out at Harvard University[80] brought out three factors which hindered a process of mourning among those who had been left behind: 1. a sudden death; 2. an ambivalent attitude to the dead person associated with guilt feelings; and 3. a dependent relationship.

Applying this finding to the situation of Peter and the disciples, we should note that all three factors which make mourning difficult to apply to them: 1. the crucifixion of Jesus happened unexpectedly and suddenly; 2. the relationship of the disciples to Jesus was marked by ambivalence and guilt feelings: Judas betrayed Jesus and then commited suicide; Peter denied Jesus and wept bitterly; 3. a dependent relationship of the disciples to Jesus can be seen in the fact that most had left their work and homes to go with him. The dependence was perhaps further intensified by the fact that the followers of Jesus represented a small religious group which had detached itself from its original social structures and thus had formally parted company with the outside world. Jesus was everything to them.

The mourning hindered by the three factors mentioned was enormously helped in the case of Peter by a 'seeing'. The mourning first led to a real, deeper understanding of Jesus, and this in turn helped toward a new understanding of the situation of mourning. Recollections of who Jesus had been led to the recognition of who Jesus *is*. Seeing Jesus thus already included a whole chain of theological conclusions.

The appearance to the twelve

In I Cor.15.5 Paul mentions the appearance to the twelve as the second seeing of Christ after the first vision of Peter's. The relationship between the two appearances can be defined in two ways.

1. The theory that both appearances go back to one presupposes that Paul would have changed an original 'Cephas and the twelve' to 'Cephas, then to the twelve', in view of the other appearances which he intended to list in order. But such a view is improbable.

2. The assumption that the appearance to Peter was an individual appearance (i.e. without the twelve) is supported by the wording of I Cor.15.5 and the suppression of the tradition of the first appearance to Peter mentioned above. Accordingly it is quite certain that the appearance to the twelve is not identical with that to Peter.

But there is no explicit report in the New Testament of the appearance to the twelve unless one connects parts of Luke 24 or John 20 with it. *But in that case – from a historical point of view – the resurrection appearance to the twelve disciples is completely obscure.*

The appearance to more than 500 brethren

The historical nucleus behind Acts 2.1–13

I hinted earlier (14ff.) that the appearance to more than 500 brethren could represent a kind of foundation legend of the Christian community and could perhaps derive from the event which historically underlies Acts 2 (= Pentecost). This supposition is not new,[81] but so far it has not become established because of 'insufficient evidence'. However, in my view one cannot avoid a renewed discussion of the thesis.

Important support comes from the following consideration: the mention of this resurrection appearance in I Cor.15 shows that it was widely known. But in that case it is very improbable that no trace should have been left of such an event before more than 500 people. Furthermore Paul emphasizes that those concerned can still be asked questions about it; only a few of them have died. So he presupposes that they have a function as witnesses which was also significant for the Christians in Corinth. This tells in favour of the general importance of this event in early Christianity.

I now want to examine the text of Acts 2.1–13 to see whether the historical resurrection appearance 'to more than 500 brethren' could lie behind it:

1. When the day of Pentecost had come, they were all together in one place.

2. And suddenly a sound came from heaven like the rush of a mighty wind, and it filled all the house where they were sitting.

3. And there appeared to them tongues as of fire, distributed and resting on each one of them.

4. And they were all filled with the Holy Spirit and began to speak in other tongues, as the Spirit gave them utterance.

5. Now there were dwelling in Jerusalem Jews, devout men from every nation under heaven.

6. And at this sound the multitude came together, and they were bewildered, because each one heard them speaking in his own language.

7. And they were amazed and wondered, saying, 'Are not all these who are speaking Galileans?

8. And how is it that we hear, each of us in his own native language?

9. Parthians and Medes and Elamites and residents of Mesopotamia, Judaea and Cappadocia, Pontus and Asia,

10. Phrygia and Pamphylia, Egypt and the parts of Libya belonging to Cyrene, and visitors from Rome, both Jews and proselytes,

11. Cretans and Arabians, we hear them telling in our own tongues the mighty works of God.'

12. And all were amazed and perplexed, saying to one another, 'What does this mean?'

13. But others mocking said, 'They are filled with new wine.'

On a first reading, the text reports a miracle involving the speaking of foreign languages on the feast of Pentecost after the death and resurrection/ascension of Jesus. The concrete indication of time, 'Pentecost',[82] indicates an earlier tradition. At the same time some tension in the text suggest existing elements of tradition. For had Luke exclusively formulated the account himself, he would have sought to eliminate inconsistencies. Thus the question arises how far Luke himself worked on the text and what he had before him.

A break in the action can be noted after v.4. The event so far has been taking place in a house and describes a 'speaking in tongues';[83] the subsequent vv.5–13 evidently depict a miracle involving foreign languages in the open air.

Both parts contain many elements of Lukan language: the house as a setting may derive from Luke, who is fond of using this motif. The mode of expression of vv.2f. has been assimilated to the revelations of God on Sinai (cf. Exod.19.16–19; Deut.4.11–12). For vv.3f. see especially Num.11.25; elsewhere, too, Luke is fond of imitating the Greek Old Testament. Furthermore, his style may be recognizable in the sevenfold 'and' used in the account. The following parallelization also suggests Luke's hand:

v.2	v.3
2. And suddenly a sound came from heaven like the rush of a mighty wind, and it filled all the house where they were sitting.	3. And there appeared to them tongues as of fire, distributed and resting on each one of them.

Within the second part (vv.5–13), the list in vv.9–11 holds back the course of the account; because of the many details and its character as a list it certainly goes back to a source. As the content and language of this material is well bound in with vv.5–13, the whole section may have been shaped by Luke, the 'and' of the previous verses 1–4 now being replaced by a recurrent 'but' (vv.5,6),7,12,13.

Other indications reinforce the impression of a Lukan composition: vv. 2–4 can stand independently, whereas the following verses presuppose vv.1–4 in the demonstrative pronouns in vv.6a ('this sound') and v.7b ('all these').

Finally, the verdict in v.13 that this is drunken talk or babbling does not fit the miraculous gift of speaking in comprehensible foreign languages very well; it is probably the original conclusion to vv.1–4. For the remark in v.4 that the disciples were speaking 'in other tongues' (= in foreign languages) seems to come from Luke himself. If we delete this one word, then behind the miracle of foreign languages as described here there is a speaking in tongues (an incomprehensible jabbering) which corresponds to that in I Cor.14 (see below).

The tradition contained in vv.1–4 (and v.13) which evidently belongs with the note of time, 'Pentecost', thus originally spoke of an ecstatic experience of the disciples of Jesus in Jerusalem, and it was Luke who interpreted it as a miracle involving the speaking of foreign languages.

The question now arises as to what hapened at Pentecost. For it is clear that here the speaking of tongues evidenced here played a central role.

The question can perhaps be answered by looking at the phenomenon of speaking with tongues attested by Paul himself. In I Cor.14.18 he claims to speak in tongues more than the Corinthians and in I Thess.5.19 ('Do not quench the spirit!')[84] seems to be encouraging his community to such talk.

Now speaking with tongues is generally incomprehensible ecstatic discourse – in the world-view of Paul, the language of angels (I Cor.13.1 [cf. II Cor.12.4]), on which I Cor.14 provides a vivid commentary: glossolalia is incomprehensible discourse (vv.2,16,23), but it can be translated and, if it is, its content is edifying (vv.4f. 26) and instructive (v.19). Either the person speaking with tongues himself or herself translates (v.13), or another member of the community is called on to do so (v.27).

A similar happening in Jerusalem is quite conceivable, and the speaking in tongues reported by the tradition underlying Acts 2.1–4.13 is historically quite plausible. Probably this event took place at Pentecost after the Passover when Jesus died, and may be identical with the appearance to more than 500 brethren (I Cor.15.6). The number 500 here is to be understood to denote 'an enormous number'.[85] Who could have counted them?

The thesis formulated at the beginning, that the appearance to more than 500 brethren is identical with the event denoted in Acts 2, may thus be regarded as fairly certain. This was an enthusiastic experience of a large crowd of people which was understood as an encounter with Christ. In view of the unusual character of such an event we must consider it quite possible that, as Luke depicts it, this is in fact to be designated the hour of the birth of the church. In that case the setting is Jerusalem, because here above all were the preconditions for a meeting of so many people – e.g. at a festival.

The appearance to more than 500 brethren – mass psychosis

Precisely how are we to imagine such an appearance to 'more than 500 brethren'? In this case there are no references to the historical context to help us to understand, similar to those that we have from their past in the case of Peter and Paul. But perhaps borrowings from research into mass psychology may help us here.

Ninety years ago, Gustav Le Bon[86] arrived at the following insight:

'People differ from one another most in intelligence, morality and ideas and least in animal instinct and emotions. Therefore the power of the mass is the greater, the more its members resemble one another, since the things in which they differ are for the moment put on one side. They then possess a kind of communal soul in which the capacities for understanding and personalities of the individuals become blurred and the unconscious properties prevail' (13f.). Le Bon further observes: 'The masses are roughly in the position of a sleeper whose capacity for thought has for the moment been removed, so that in his spirit images of the most extreme vigour arise, but quickly vanish away once reflection has had a say' (43). Everything that stimulates the imagination of the masses is said to appear in the form of a gripping, clear image which needs no interpretation (44). Here one could even say that the members of a mass have an infectious influence on one another.[87]

Le Bon cites the following instructive example of this infectious influence:

Before St George appeared to all the crusaders on the walls of Jerusalem he was first certainly perceived by only some of them. Through influence and transference the miracle thus proclaimed was immediately accepted by all. Thus there came about the process of colletive hallucinations which are so frequent in history and seem to have classical characteristics of authenticity, as here we have appearances which were noted by thousands of people (23f.).

In all such mass phenomena we have psychological processes, but that is not to say anything about their significance and truth content. Just as God's Word can appear, for example, in human speech without being absorbed in it, so too a psychological event may be the human context of an appearance of the divine Spirit. History or psychology and theology relate to each other, since they relate to diferent aspects of the one reality, but they cannot be reduced to each other. Here we are first of all concerned with the historical aspect.

What happened at Pentecost

The appearance to 'more than 500' as a historical phenomenon can plausibly be represented as mass ecstasy which took place in the early period of the community. From the perspective of mass psychology, one or more individuals may have been the catalyst for such ecstasy. Again that fits well with what has been worked out so far, namely that at least a first appearance took place to Peter (and to the twelve): Peter saw the crucified Jesus alive (as did the twelve). They also spoke of it, for example, at the next great festival (after the Passover at which Jesus died) in Jerusalem, the Jewish feast of weeks (= Pentecost), on which many festival pilgrims had met. Such a festival is in fact a prior condition for an appearance to a larger number of people.

This preaching, and general recollections of Jesus, led to religious intoxication and an enthusiasm which was experienced as the presence of Jesus, indeed as the presence of the Risen Christ as he had already encountered Peter. The appearance to the 'more than 500', at which those who had previously received visions were also present, brought together and confirmed all previous individual experiences and thus gave the group an incomparable thrust.[88]

In retrospect, and with historical appropriateness, Luke then spoke of this as the 'hour of the birth of the church' and – similarly with theological justification – interpreted the ecstasy as a capacity to speak comprehensibly in foreign languages. For the message represented by Jesus meant something to all people. Had there been no more than ecstasy and intoxication, Christianity would have had no chance of survival and could not have asserted itself. But also, theologically speaking, it would not have remained faithful to its task of addressing God's saving word to human beings in comprehensible language.

I am not asserting here that this is the only course that the events could have followed. But I am claiming that these reflections have developed a historical notion of the event which is appropriate to the sources and the conclusions that can be drawn from them.

The appearance to James (and all the apostles[89])

An appearance of the Risen Christ to his brother James is not described in the New Testament anywhere other than in I Corinthians. However, it is described in the Gospel of the Hebrews[90] as follows:

> And when the Lord had given the linen cloth to the servant of the priest, he went to James and appeared to him. For James had sworn that he would not eat bread from that hour in which he had drunk the cup of the Lord until he should see him risen from among them that sleep. And shortly thereafter the Lord said: Bring a table and bread! And immediately it is added: he took the bread, blessed it and brake it and gave it to James the Just and said to him: 'My brother, eat your bread, for the Son of man is risen from among them that sleep.'[91]

The text has the following peculiarities relating to the person of James: (a) James is the first witness to the resurrection; (b) already before Easter James belonged to the community; (c) the focal point of the text is the release of James from a vow, not the reality of the resurrection of Jesus or an appearance of Christ. Perhaps here the vow is modelled on Peter's promise to go with his Lord to death (Mark 14.31). If James had fulfilled the vow, while Peter was known to have broken it, the first testimony would emphatically have to be attributed to James. (d) However, little can be traced of any *direct* rivalry with other apostles or Peter (in the text) despite (c); indeed, neither Peter nor other disciples are mentioned at all.

These statements are already a long way from historical reality: James (not Jesus) stands at the centre, and the fact that he was not one of the disciples in the time of Jesus is forgotten.

Furthermore, the attestation to the report is late. Its basis is a New Testament tradition of the eucharist which has been transformed into a personal legend to glorify James. Apart from the fact that Jesus appeared to James, the text gives us no reliable information. Rather, it serves to enable admirers of James in the second and third generations to claim the first appearance for James rather than Cephas/Peter.[92]

It follows from all this that the report of the Gospel of the Hebrews has been shaped at a later date on the basis of already existing traditions of appearances and certainly does not go back to the attestation of James or his immediate followers. It is exclusively a literary product and has no relationship to the real, historical appearance to James.

Only vague conjectures are possible about the historical background to this individual vision, which must have represented a kind of conversion of James. Because of I Cor.15.7 it is certain that James 'saw' his brother. But this could primarily have been within the framework of the appearance to more than 500 brethren, which was then possibly followed by an individual vision. It should be noted that James had no religious link with his brother during Jesus' lifetime. The presuppositions for a vision were therefore different from those in Peter's case. That James later became leader of the earliest community has more to do with the fact that he was a member of the family, since in antiquity people thought in terms of family politics. Similarly Symeon, also a relative of Jesus, became James' successor to the 'see of Jerusalem' (cf. above, 42f.).[93]

The appearance to Paul

Paul himself does not give a concrete description anywhere of the way in which he really experienced the appearance of the risen Christ. He always presupposes what once happened to him on his way to Damascus. Only through this appearance was he entrusted with the mission to the Gentiles, thus having his actions legitimated once and for all.

Paul mentions his experience of Christ in the following texts: I Cor.9.1; Gal.1.15f.; Phil.3.8; II Cor.4.6. We shall deal with the passages from the letters of Paul in order. Our starting point here is that some characteristics of the event can be extracted from these retrospects of Paul over twenty years and despite current problems in the churches which may also have influenced his retrospective statements about his conversion.

I Corinthians 9.1

In I Cor.9.1 Paul says that he has *seen* Jesus (cf. John 20.18,25).

> 1. Am I not free? Am I not an apostle? Have I not seen Jesus our Lord? Are you not my workmanship in the Lord?

Here Paul uses an active form of the verb 'see'. Thus he is expressing as his own active sensual perception the same substantive content as in I Cor.15.8, without resorting to possible appearance or legitimation formulae. So Paul is claiming a visual side to the appearance mentioned in I Cor.15.8. In that case I Cor.9.1 is the active perception of Jesus, for which the appearance stated in I Cor.15.8 is the presupposiiton.

In my view it is certain that here the apostle is thinking of a vision of Jesus in his transformed spiritual resurrection corporeality. Otherwise it would be hard to understand how Paul could refer to 'seeing' (I Cor.15.4ff.) for the certainty of the bodily resurrection. It is important, though, that Paul does not equate the two. Therefore in I Cor.15.35–49 he speaks of a future resurrection body of Christians. Similarly Paul may also have assumed a (transformed) resurrection body of Jesus, all the more so since he accepts the principle: as Christ, so Christians (cf. I Cor.15.29; Phil.3.21).

Galatians 1.15f.

In Galatians Paul uses another verb to describe the same appearance. In Gal.1.15f. he writes:

> 15. When he who had set me apart before I was born, and had called me through his grace,
> 16. was pleased to reveal his son to me, in order that I might preach him among the Gentiles . . .

Thus God is the one who is active in 'revealing' his Son in/to Paul. This statement might be referring to a particular event. Here v.12 ('For I did not receive it from man, nor was I taught it, but it came through a revelation of Jesus Christ') makes it clear in connection with v.16 that the content of the event was a revelation which had Christ either as the subject or the author. At all events, the motif of revelation fits the seeing in I Cor.9.1 and its presupposition, the appearance in I Cor.15.8.

Here the terms 'revelation' and 'appearance' or 'see' are not mutually exclusive. 'Revelation' denotes an experience of a *religious* kind as coming directly from God, 'appearance' describes it in its *spatial* aspect. By a shift in vocabulary Paul is emphasizing different aspects of the same thing.

Philippians 3.8

In Philippians 3.8 Paul again speaks of his 'appearance experience':

> 7. But whatever gain I had, I counted as loss for the sake of Christ. 8. Indeed, I count everything as loss because of the surpassing worth of knowing Christ Jesus my Lord. For his sake I have suffered the loss of all things, and count them as refuse, in order that I may gain Christ . . .

Here the apostle is speaking of the 'knowledge' of Christ which has led him to see his life hitherto as 'refuse'. The whole section (vv.2–11) is markedly polemical. As already in Gal.1.13f., Paul emphasizes his unobjectionable life as a Jew (vv.4–6) and distinguishes from it the righteousness from faith that was revealed to him by the knowledge of Christ (v.9). So here again there is a theological interpretation of the appearance of Christ before Damascus and only a sparse description of what *really* happened at the time. So it is not the case historically, as has sometimes been claimed, that there is no visionary element in Phil.3. The question to be put in the historical framework is whether the visionary element of the revelation attested in other passages is excluded here. But there can be no question of that: I Cor.9.1 (Paul sees the risen Jesus) explains how the polemical statements in Phil.3.4ff. can be understood historically.

II Corinthians 4.6

Finally, in II Cor.4.6 we have yet another possible reference to the appearance of Christ:

> 6. For it is the God who said, 'Let light shine out of darkness', who has shone in our hearts to give the light of the knowledge of the glory of God in the face of Christ.

Should this passage refer to Paul's conversion, which is admittedly uncertain, it would be probable that at this conversion Paul saw Christ in the form of light. This would fit the remarks in I Cor.15.49 about the heavenly man ('Just as we have born the image or the man of dust, we shall also bear the image of the man of heaven'). Paul would then be putting his vision of Christ in parallel with the dawning of light on creation morning, to express what had happened to him.

So specifically, 'Jesus appeared to Paul' means that Paul saw the risen Jesus in his glory, which need not tell against an inner vision of the outward vision. This vision was felt to be an extraordinary event and a revelation. This is expressed by the character of the event as 'light'. Like the vision of the seer John (Rev.1.10), it took place in the spirit, i.e. in rapture/ecstasy.[94] In it, seeing and hearing were not mutually exclusive.

Thus far our provisional description of the appearance to Paul. On the basis of the identification of all the persons (above, 82f.) who according to the other traditions in I Cor.15.3ff. were granted an appearance of the risen Jesus, that means that *the people mentioned there also saw the risen Jesus.*

The appearance of the risen Christ to Paul according to Acts 9; 22; 26

The appearance to Paul is not mentioned only in Paul's letters. There are also passages in Acts which report at length this appearance, which for Paul was a conversion experience. But we must be very critical in using them to illuminate events.

Acts was written relatively late (around 90). Its author, who was also the author of the Gospel of Luke, emphasizes the continuity between the beginning in Palestinian Jewish Christianity and his own situation in a Gentile Christian church. He therefore offers an account with an orientation on salvation history, leading to the worldwide mission to the Gentiles. Here situations are improved and events harmonized. Nevertheless the historical value of the traditions used in Acts is high. However, careful exegetical work is necessary for us to be able to use its traditions.

So in this connection the letters of Paul must always be consulted as a check on what is said in Acts. Were the Acts statements confirmed by the authentic testimony of the letters, we would have a broader basis for giving a closer definition of the appearances of the risen Christ before Damascus.

Acts reports the conversion of Paul/Saul at three points.[95] A comparison makes it clear that they belong together. Acts 9 (with 8.3) has an account in the third person, Acts 22 and 26 in the first person: in 22.3–16 Paul is giving a speech in the temple to fellow countrymen, in 26.9–18 he is speaking to Agrippa, Festus and Berenice.

Acts (8.3) 9.1–19	Acts 22.4–16	Acts 26.9–18
8.3 But Saul laid waste the church, and entering house after house, he dragged off men and women and committed them to prison.	22.4 I persecuted this Way to the death, binding and delivering to prison both men and women,	26.9 I myself was convinced that I ought to do many things in opposing the name of Jesus of Nazareth. 10. And I did so in Jerusalem; I not only shut up many of the saints in prison,
9.1 But Saul, still breathing threats and murder against the disciples of the Lord,		
	5. as the high priest and the whole council of elders bear me witness.	by authority from the chief priests, but when they were put to death I cast my vote against them. 11. And I punished them in all the synagogues and tried to make

went to the high priest 2. and asked him for letters to the synagogues at Damascus, so that if he found any belonging to the Way, men or women, he might bring them bound to Jerusalem. 3. Now as he journeyed, he approached Damascus,

and suddenly a light from heaven flashed about him.

4. And he fell to the ground and heard a voice

saying to me, 'Saul, Saul, why do you persecute me?'

From them I received letters to the brethren, and I journeyed to Damascus to take those also who were there and bring them in bonds to Jerusalem to be punished. 6. As I made my journey and drew near to Damascus,

about noon a great light from heaven suddenly shone about me

7. And I fell to the ground and hear a voice

saying to me, 'Saul, Saul, why do you persecute me?'

them blaspheme, and in raging fury against them, I persecuted them even to foreign cities. 12. Thus I journeyed to Damascus with the authority and commission of the chief priests.

13. At midday, O king, I saw on the way a light from heaven, brighter than the sun, shining round me and those who journeyed with me. 14. And when we had all fallen to the ground, I heard a voice saying to me in the Hebrew language, 'Saul, Saul, why do you persecute me? It hurts you to kick against the goads.

5. And he said, 'Who are you, Lord?' And he answered, 'I am Jesus,

whom you are persecuting.

7. The men who were travelling with him stood speechless, hearing the voice but seeing no one.

(6 *but rise and enter the city, and you will be told what you are to do.*)

8. Saul arose from the ground; and when his eyes were opened, he could see nothing; so they led him by the hand and brought him into Damascus.

9. And for three days he was without sight, and neither ate nor drank.

8. And I answered, 'Who are you, Lord?' And he said to me, 'I am Jesus of Nazareth whom you are persecuting.'

9. Now those who were with me saw the light but did not hear the voice of the one who was speaking to me.

10. And I said, 'What shall I do, Lord?' And the Lord said to me:

'Rise, and go into Damascus, and there you will be told all that is appointed for you to do.'

11. And when I could not see because of the brightness of that light, I was led by the hand by those who were with me, and came into Damascus.

15. And I said, 'Who are you, Lord?' And the Lord said, 'I am Jesus

whom you are persecuting.

But rise and stand upon your feet;

10. Now there was a disciple at Damascus named Ananias.

The Lord said to him in a vision, 'Ananias.' and he said, 'Here I am Lord,' 11. And the Lord said to him, 'Rise and go to the street called Straight, and inquire in the house of Judas for a man of Tarsus named Saul; for behold, he is praying, 12. and he has seen a man named Ananias come in and lay his hands on him so that he might regain his sight. 13. But Ananias answered, 'Lord, I have heard from many about this man, how much evil he has done to your saints at Jerusalem; and here he has authority from the chief priest to bind all who call upon your name.'

12. And one Ananias, a devout man according to the law, well spoken of by all the Jews who lived there.

15. But the Lord said to him, 'Go, for he is a chosen instrument of mine

(14. *And he said, The God of our fathers has appointed you to know his will and to hear a voice from his mouth;* 15. *for you will be a witness to all men of what you have seen and heard.*)

for I have appeared to you for this purpose, to appoint you to serve

and bear witness to the things in which you have seen me and to those in which I will appear to you, 17. delivering you from the people and from the Gentiles — to whom I send you, 18. to open their eyes, that they may turn from darkness to light and from the power of Satan to God, that they may receive forgiveness of sins and a place among those who are sanctified by faith in me.'

to carry my name before the Gentiles and the kings and the sons of Israel;

16. for I will show him how much he must suffer for the sake of my name.'

17. So Ananias departed and entered the house. And laying hands on him he said, 'Brother Saul, the

13. He came to me, and standing by me, said to me, 'Brother Saul,

Lord Jesus who
appeared to you on
the road by which you
came, has sent me
that you may regain   receive your sight.'
your sight and be
filled with the Holy
Spirit.' 18. And   And in that very
immediately some-   hour
thing
like scales fell from
his eyes and he   I received my
regained his sight.   sight and saw him.
                            16. 'And now, why
Then he rose and was   do you wait? Rise
baptized,   and be baptized,
                            and wash away your
19. and took food   sins, calling
and was   on his name.'
strengthened.

All three accounts say that Saul has Christians put in prison (Acts 8.3; 22.4; 26.9–11); in Acts 26 this statement is further heightened: Paul's acts of persecution are extended to distant cities (26.11b). All of the accounts mention letters which Saul asks for (9.2) or has received (22.5b; 26.12) from the high priest in order to be able to persecute Christians in Damascus as well.

The actual appearance is mentioned in 9.3–9; 22.6–11 and 26.12–16a. I shall use Acts 9 as the main text for a comparison with the two other accounts, because it is the most extensive.

9.1–2 represents the introduction to the following narrative of the appearance. After taking part in the stoning of Stephen (7.58; 8.1a) and subsequently successfully persecuting Christians (8.3) – both episodes have been shaped by Luke – Saul wants to extend his hunt of Christians geographically. The appearance of Christ then takes place on the way to Damascus. This skilfully creates a contrast between the zealous persecutor of Christians and the convert.

9.3 corresponds down to its vocabulary with 22.6. However, the verse contains no note of time, whereas 22.6 speaks of 'around midday' and 26.13 similarly of 'in the middle of the day'. Here the introduction in v.3a ('as he journeyed') derives from Luke, who introduces an episode in a similar way at Acts 10.9; Luke 18.35; 19.29.

In all three accounts the appearance to Saul is described as light. 26.13 intensifies this by saying that the light is brighter than the rays of the sun (hence the mention of midday). In 9.3 and 22.6 the light shines (only) around Saul; in 26.13 it shines round Saul and his companions. 9.3 and 22.6 make the appearance take place 'suddenly'.

Verses 4b–6 may be described as an 'appearance conversation', which is contained within the three accounts of the conversion of Saul, also in 22.7–10 and 26.14–16; it has parallels in the Old Testament: Gen.31.11–13; 46.2f.; Ex.3.2–10. The Old Testament 'appearance conversations' all have a tripartite structure:

1. Address or call,
2. response,
3. introduction with command.

It is probable that Luke has also imitated this form here: he uses the tripartite form elsewhere. That it comes from Luke himself is reinforced by two further indications: 1. vv.4b–6 are not necessary for the action; 2. Luke has a fondness for creating scenes with dialogues.

According to 9.4 and 22.7 Saul falls to the ground: in 26.14 so do his companions. All three narratives agree that Saul hears a voice which says to him, 'Saul, Saul, why are you persecuting me?' This duplication goes back to Luke and has a parallel in the address of Luke 8.24 (Mark differs), 10.41 and 22.31.

By contrast, 26.14 has two interesting additions: 1. the voice speaks in Hebrew; 2. the question to Saul as to why he is persecuting the speaker is supplemented by the comment, 'It hurts you to kick against the goads'. These two additions are Lukan expansions. The first addition (the Hebrew language) is to explain to the reader of Acts the Hebrew form of the name 'Saul', which appears in all three versions. However, the fact that in the second addition the persecuted Jeus quotes a Greek proverb does not fit the Hebrew language. Here in fact the writer Luke is speaking; he wants on the one hand to demonstrate the complete dependence of Saul on Jesus, and on the other to show off his wide reading.

9.5 corresponds almost completely with the parallels 22.8 and 26.15.

9.6 corresponds to 22.10. By contrast, 26.16 contains simply an order to rise and immediately describes the real command to Saul to preach, which the parallel versions give only later (in 9.15; 22.15). Therefore in the following verse only 9.7–9 and 22.9–11 can be compared.

The statement in 9.7 that Paul's companions heard the voice but did not see the light conflicts with 22.9, where the opposite is said: the companions saw the light but did not hear the voice.

9.8 corresponds to 22.11.

9.9 has no parallel in ch.22. The observation that Saul could not see anything for three days and did not eat and drink is perhaps an addition. At all events three is a symbolic number (for Luke).

In 9.10–17 a vision of Christ to Ananias is depicted as the prelude to his later encounter with Paul. For Luke, visions are an important literary means for communicating divine decisions (cf. e.g. Acts 10f.; 16.9f.; 18.9f.). Here the introduction of Ananias takes place in Lukan language (cf. Luke 10.38; 16.20; Acts 5.1; 8.9; 10.1, etc.).

In 22.12, however, Ananias is introduced only briefly. The healing of Saul takes place soon afterwards (v.13), whereas in ch.9 it is related only in the later v.17. The introduction of Ananias in 22.12 without further elucidation of the prehistory of his intervention is abrupt, and can happen only because the readers have already learned something about him in ch.9. So ch.22 refers back to ch.9. Chapter 26 continues the abbreviation of the account and completely passes over the Ananias episode.

As in the preceding narrative of Philip and the Ethiopian eunuch (8.26–40) and the story of Cornelius (Acts 10), here in 9.10–16 the actions of the two figures are interwoven through appearances. This should make it clear that the development of the action in this section of Acts is increasingly governed by divine intervention. The three accounts are thus combined by Luke to form a progression.

9.15–16 has a parallel in 22.14–15 and 26.16b. However, different accents are clear: 9.15 designates Saul a 'chosen instrument' of the Lord for mission and gives the basis for this statement in v.16: Saul is marked out as a future martyr.

The situation in ch.22 and especially ch.26 is different from this. 22.14 has a different subject from 9.13: God has chosen Saul. The second part of 9.14 has no parallel in 9.15 or 26.16. But with 26.16 there is a parallel with regard to the seeing/appearance of Jesus.

9.17–19 depicts the healing of Saul by Ananias, which is reported at an earlier stage in ch.22, at v.13.

In addition to ch.9 there is a close parallel to 22.15 in 26.16b: according to both versions Saul is a witness. The special task of the witness is developed in 26.17–18 (without a parallel in ch.32). Here the calling of Saul to be a missionary to the Gentiles is expressed, a theme which is not in ch.9 and only indirectly in ch.22.1–16.

All three accounts of the appearance to Paul which have been considered belong together. At the level of their origin, the second account in 22.12 presupposes the first, just as the third version (26.9ff.) can be understood as an abbreviation of the previous two. In the third version the contrast between Paul's pre-Christian and Christian periods (cf. the elaboration of Paul's activity as a persecutor) is intensified and the conversion of Acts 9 is seen as a call to the Gentile mission.

So in what follows we shall keep to the first and most extensive text, Acts 9. The two parallel accounts in Acts 22 and 26 do not contain any further information.

A. *The traditions behind Acts 9.3–8*

It should be noted that vv.4b–6 in this form certainly come from Luke, but they possibly have a basis in tradition. Moreover it remains uncertain whether elements of the tradition have been deleted by Luke. The following elements of tradition can certainly be made out.

1. Saul, the persecutor of Christians, is near Damascus.
2. A heavenly light shines out and Saul falls down.
3. His companions, who have heard the voice speaking to Saul, take him (blinded?) to Damascus.

Reconstructed in this way, the tradition can be described as a legend of the punishment of someone who despises God. Saul understood his call to mission (among the Gentiles) as being a result of it.

For Luke, however, Paul's mission is not yet a theme in the scheme of Acts as early as ch.9. Accordingly, at that point he has probably deliberately interpreted the tradition of a calling of Paul (cf. Acts 22 and 26) as a conversion and put it in a series of three conversion stories (8.26–40; 9.1–19a; 10.1–11.18). The tradition of the Damascus event which Luke had was probably originally the story of a calling which essentially corresponds with Paul's own testimony. For descriptive reasons Luke has triplicated it and in Acts 9 has moved away from historical truth to some degree by interpreting the calling as a conversion.

In agreement with Paul's letters, the tradition reports with historical accuracy that a particular event made the persecutor a proclaimer, the enemy of Christ a disciple of Christ (cf. Gal.1).

Furthermore, the information that the conversion or calling took place in or near Damascus is also accurate. In Gal.1.17 Paul himself also says that he went to Arabia in connection with the conversion and then returned to Damascus. So he must have been in or near this city soon after his conversion.

We may also consider whether the basis of the tradition in Acts 9.3–9 itself comes from Damascus. Furthermore, we may see one of the starting points for the tradition in Gal.1.23 ('He who once persecuted us is now preaching the faith he once tried to destroy'). Nor should Paul's contribution to the formation of the tradition about his 'change' be underestimated: he himself will doubtless have described it.

At this point one might also ask whether Saul's blindness was an element of the tradition. Examples of ecstatic blindness are known in history. Here the decisive question will be whether the evidence itself gives further indications that blindness was associated with the Damascus event (see below 118f.).

B. The tradition behind Acts 9.10–19

It is even more difficult to determine any basis of tradition underlying the section vv.10–19. Probably the only element of tradition is the disciple Ananias in Damascus, who healed and perhaps also baptized Paul there (9.18); Luke will hardly have added this name to the tradition. Whether the house of Judas in the street called Straight is part of the tradition is unclear.

Paul's 'Easter'

The tradition behind Acts 9.3–9 agrees with Paul's own testimonies in reporting a resurrection appearance. In I Cor.9.1f. Paul speaks in 'Easter language' (cf. John 20.18,25) of seeing the Lord, and similarly in I Cor.15.8 of Jesus showing himself to him (Luke 24.34; I Cor.15.3–7). Both passages reflect one and the same event; here I Cor.9.1 formulates the active perception of Jesus and I Cor.15.8 its presupposition.

However, what is said about the appearance of Christ in Acts 9.3–9 and in the letters of Paul also differs. Acts does not explicitly speak of 'seeing' the Lord (thus the letters) but of hearing his words (vv.4b–6) and of a light shining from heaven and Paul's falling down. At all events, vv.3–9 say nothing about Saul having seen the Lord.

By comparison, however, we might refer to Acts 9.17, where Ananias, looking back on vv.3–9, describes the appearance of light before Damascus as an appearance of Jesus to Saul (cf.26.19), and to 9.7 (his companions saw no one). This probably presupposes that Saul saw someone, i.e. Jesus.

So there is no conflict over the mode of Jesus' appearance between 9.3–9 and the letters of Paul: both attest that Paul saw Jesus. Johannes Lindblom rightly calls the Damascus event a 'vivid vision with a strong auditive element',[96] i.e. hearing also played a role.

Paul himself indicates that the appearance before Damascus called him to be a missionary (cf. esp. Gal.1.15f.). That is not said in Acts 9. However, this can be explained simply from the narrative intention of the tradition (or of Luke?), which (or who) at this point puts the emphasis wholly on the overcoming of the persecutor of Christians by Jesus. On the other hand the call of Paul the persecutor to be a missionary introduces a conclusive shift which is described in Acts 9. So it is quite possible that what Luke has narrated in Acts 9 and 26 in two stories with different focal points in fact took place historically within a short space of time (Acts 22 comes in between). In that case Acts 9 and 26 simply contain different aspects of the same event.

It is probably hardly possible to make any well-founded historical judgment on the person of Ananias and his involvement in the conversion/calling of Saul. However, it is illegitimate to cite Gal.1.12, that Paul does not have his revelation from a human person, against any involvement of Ananias in whatever form. For this information hardly excludes the involvement of Ananias, as it would not put in question the particular character of the conversion/ call, and Ananias would have to be regarded as an instrument of God.

The most important result of the historical reconstruction of the appearance to Paul is the insight that Paul's own testimony and what is said in Acts essentially agree. Thus the accounts in Acts enrich our historical knowledge of Paul's experience of Christ. *The tradition worked over by Luke may go back to an account from the apostle himself. It contains details which are already to be noted in the letters of Paul.*

However, by way of qualification it should be said that we can no longer determine whether the aspect of call in the Damascus event was part of the event itself. It is probable that the understanding of the conversion as a call first derived from an interpretation by Paul which may have been made subsequently, albeit within a short period.

We need to maintain that *Paul 'saw' Jesus in the event before Damascus. Whether we call this a 'conversion' or not is relatively unimportant, as the content is clear: Paul did a U-turn from being a persecutor to proclaiming Jesus.* A revolution of values took place within his own person, from the Jewish law to Christ.

The appearance of Christ to Paul: A vision?

The 'Damascus event' has the characteristic of a vision. ' "Visions" are usually understood to be appearances of figures, things or events, or perceptions of voices and sounds which have no objective reality for the senses, but according to those who see and hear them come from another, invisible world.'[97] Thus a 'vision' is initially a neutral phenomenon. Only in its interpretation by the visionary or by an outsider does it take on a 'negative' (or even a 'positive') tendency. Thus the term 'vision' is used in connection with Paul's experience of an appearance (and also for Peter's experience) to indicate that he experienced something, saw (and heard) something, which *he* could not explain as being 'of this world'.

There are examples of visions in the Old Testament,[98] in Judaism at the beginning of the Common Era,[99] in numerous parallels from the Hellenistic and Roman environment of the New Testament[100] and in the New Testament itself.[101]

In reading the most recent book on Easter by Hans Kessler, one gets an impression of the resurrection appearances which cannot be contradicted emphatically enough. This is what Kessler says:

> The view . . . that these are visions that can be explained in purely psychological terms, in other words as mere products of the imagination or subconscious of the disciples, must be excluded . . . There are no indications whatsoever that early Christianity derived Easter faith from inner psychological events. And in any case a purely psychological explanation fails to do justice to the seriousness, the religious claim of the texts.[102]

This view does not do justice to the phenomenon, since it does not matter to a scientific account of the 'Easter events' whether early Christianity derived the Easter faith from inner events within the soul or not. Nor could the first Christians have expressed such an experience, since the ancient world-view hardly distinguished between 'purely inward' and 'purely external' events. At that time visions were part of 'normal' daily life and were regarded as mysterious, inexplicable phenomena produced by higher beings. So we of today must be concerned to provide an approach to the Easter event which can be understood *today*. First of all, therefore, we must ask whether a psychological approach helps us to understand the religious earnestness of the visionaries of the time. And this cannot easily be disputed.

Carl Holsten discusses the general conditions and possibilities of visions.[103] He writes that there can be visions only 'where the elements of the vision were already present in the spirit of the visionary. The visionary imagination is a reproductive activity; what is seen is only what is already lived as a notion or an image of the free imagination in the consciousness of the visionary' (81f.). With reference to Paul this means:

> Criticism must be able to demonstrate that the vision of the Messiah in the form in which Paul saw it did not contradict his general world-view, that in its substantial content it had already previously been in his consciousness and conscious imagination, that it corresponded to the particular situation in which we must think Paul to have been at the time of the vision, and as a result that it was a significant image for him (84).

Holsten believes that he can demonstrate all these conditions on the basis of Paul's individuality. In his view, Paul was an epileptic and had an extremely excitable and restless character (76f.). To this 'natural determination', which in itself already reacted sensitively to external influences, was also added an above average spiritual vigour. For the conversion of Paul by his experience of Christ before Damascus, this means that by his persecution of the Christian community Paul got to know their faith in the crucified Christ. Here their unshakable faith in the redemptive power of someone who had been executed, which seemed to him as a Jew to be absurd, surprised him. This external fact occupied Paul so much that finally the significance of the crucifixion of the Messiah dawned on him as a religious necessity. The Jewish ideal of the Messiah as a national redeemer was replaced by a new view of the work of the Messiah which had extinguished all national features. Thus the Christ event before Paul was shown to be the product of a human spirit seeking knowledge (cf. 121).

In order to become clear about this we need to answer the question whether Paul had any visions elsewhere. Is even Eduard Meyer right in saying that the apostle continually experienced visions and revelations similar to those in II Cor.12?[104] If that were the case, the appearance of Christ to Paul would not be an individual instance without parallels (note that we are not concerned with the *content* of visions here but with the *fact* of visions in the life of Paul generally).

It has to be said that there is often vigorous resistance to calling Paul a 'visionary'. But it seems that all such objections are based on an inability to perceive and accept the piety or the religious life of Paul as it was.[105] The reasons for this lie in resistance to accepting that Paul's spirituality could have been other than one's own. Has modern Protestant theology and exegesis even an 'anti-visionary complex'?

But enough of conjectures and questions. I shall use a specific text, II Cor.12, to see whether visions were also important for Paul in his Christian period, and if so, attempt to determine the relationship between this passage and the Damascus vision.

II Corinthians 12.1–10

In II Cor.10.12–12.18 Paul rejects a charge, apparently that he is not sufficiently endowed with the spirit of God.

12.1 I must boast; there is nothing to be gained for it, but I will go on to visions and revelations of the Lord.

2. I know a man in Christ who fourteen years ago was caught up to the third heaven – whether in the body or out of the body I do not know, God knows.

3. And I know that this man was caught up into paradise – whether in the body or out of the body I do not know, God knows –

4. and he heard things that cannot be told, which man may not utter.

5. On behalf of this man I will boast, but on my own behalf I will not boast, except of my weakness.

6. Though if I wish to boast I shall not be a fool, for I shall be speaking the truth. But I refrain from it, so that no one may think more of me than he sees in me or hears from me.

7. And to keep me from being too elated by the abundance of revelations, a thorn was given me in the flesh, a messenger of Satan, to harass me, to keep me from being too elated.

8. Three times I besought the Lord about this, that it should leave me;

9. but he said to me, 'My grace is sufficient for you, for my power is made perfect in weakness.' I will all the more gladly boast of my weaknesses, that the power of Christ may rest upon me.

10. For the sake of Christ, then, I am content with weaknesses, insults, hardships, persecutions, and calamities; for when I am weak, then I am strong.

We know from Paul himself that there was polemic against him in Corinth. He was said to be servile in the presence of the Corinthians, but bold when away from them (II Cor.10.1, probably a quotation). II Corinthians 10.10 ('For they say, "His letters are weighty and strong, but his bodily presence is weak, and his speech of no account"') confirms this. The last-mentioned charge recurs in II Cor.11.6: Paul is said to be 'unskilled in speaking'; this certainly does not mean a lack of rhetorical training but a lack of effective speech inspired by the Spirit.

Paul's opponents in II Cor.13.3 are to be identified as 'pneumatics', i.e. as persons who are in possession of the Holy Spirit.[106] This speaks through them and enables them to perform actions brought about by the spirit.

3. You desire proof that Christ is speaking in me. He is not weak in dealing with you but powerful in you.

The opponents are evidently requiring proof that the Holy Spirit is also at work in Paul. Until this is given, they will criticize him for not being sufficiently 'pneumatic'.

When Paul writes in II Cor.12.1b 'but I will go on to visions and revelations of the Lord', he is thus taking up an accusation made against him. In II Cor.12.2–8 he is seeking to demonstrate that he, too, can boast of visions and revelations of the Lord. Evidently part of the charge of weakness (II Cor.10.10) was that Paul could not demonstrate such things. So the section is part of an argument against opponents about whom we have only limited knowledge. We must therefore be very careful about trying to derive any historical information from it.

[1a] 'I must boast' takes up II Cor.11.30a ('If I must boast'), where there is a reference to the need to boast of weakness. There, after an oath (v.31, cf. Gal.1.20), Paul tells of his flight from Damascus (vv.32–33). This is evidently meant to illustrate his weakness (vv.5b, 9).

[1b] 'Visions' and 'revelation' are almost synonymous. We might start from the hypothesis that visions can be understood as seeing and revelation as hearing (cf. Dan.10.1). However, 'revelation' takes place not only in words but also in inner illumination (cf. I Cor.14.6,26).

[2–4] Paul writes in the third person, although he is talking about himself. By using this style the apostle gives his remarks an objective character and at the same time maintains a modest approach.

The precise detail 'fourteen years ago' emphasizes the truth in the events that are to be described. The dating of the call visions of the Old Testament prophets (Isa 6.1; Jer.1.1ff.; 26.1ff., etc.) probably has a similar function. The only difference is that Paul uses the note of time, not in connection with his call but in controversy with his opponents. But in both instances the vital question is what actually happened.

Verses 2 and 3f. have a parallel structure:

v.2	v.3
I know a man in Christ who fourteen years ago was caught up to the	And I know that this man was caught up into paradise

third heaven
whether in the body	whether in the body
or out of the body I	or out of the body I
do not know, God knows.	do not know, God knows –

Either, as most exegetes assume, vv.3f. are a variant of v.2 – in which
case third heaven would be identical with paradise – or vv.3f.
contain a second heavenly journey, into paradise above the third
heaven. Because of the strikingly parallel formulation, preference is
to be given to the first of the two possibilities, especially since in
Judaism paradise could also be located in the third heaven (otherwise
it is in the seventh heaven).[107] If we have two different events here,
then only one note of time would be hardly comprehensible. So in
vv.2–4 Paul is depicting a single heavenly journey which has many
parallels in the environment of early Christianity. The repetition of
the narrative emphasizes the extraordinary event and the note of
time the truthfulness of the report.

The journey to heaven or rapture described by Paul anticipated for
a moment the 'going home' to the Lord (= dying) which Paul
hoped for so deeply in Phil.1.21 ('For to me to live is Christ and to die
is gain', cf. II Cor.5.1f.,6–8). Here he did not know whether he was
'in the body or out of the body'. Visionaries 'often have the
awareness . . . of experiencing their ecstasy in the form of a bodily
rapture . . .'[108] The clause 'God alone knows' which is added
immediately indicates that the event is caused by God – out of grace
(see also II Cor.5.1). Although Paul does not describe the circumstances more closely, we are justified in assuming that the heavenly
journey was bound up with some form of ecstasy. In keeping with
that, he speaks of himself in the third person. 'The one enraptured in
ecstasy distinguishes himself from ordinary people and speaks of
himself as though he were someone else.'[109] Since for Paul the result
of this experience was a temporary communion with the heavenly
Christ – anticipating the eschatological communion – and on the
other hand for him the Lord is the Spirit (II Cor.3.17; Rom.8.9f.), it
can be said that in *II Cor.12 Paul is describing ecstasy as a pneumatic
experience.*

In Jewish and Greek accounts of ascensions, what the persons
concerned saw and heard is often reported in greater or lesser detail.
By contrast, Paul merely says that he 'heard things that cannot be
told'. That can mean either words which cannot be told or words

which may not be told. Because of the continuation 'which man may not utter . . .', the second possibility is to be preferred.

Paul does not say whether he *saw* anything or, if he did, what it was. However, he hints at this with the word 'paradise'. He felt the place where the 'journey' ended to be paradise, and he will have 'known', i.e. probably also seen, what there was in paradise. 'Above all in addition to angels and the righteous he will have seen "the Lord" himself in this place on his throne, Acts 7.56: Rev.1.9ff.'[110] However, it should be emphasized once again that there is no explicit mention of any seeing in the present text. Still, it should probably be presupposed.[111] Furthermore, that seeing and hearing belong together is also suggested in this context by the great wealth of imagery which the visionary language contains.

[5] As far as the visionary Paul endowed by God is concerned, Paul wants to boast of this man. As far as it concerns himself as Paul the 'normal human being', he wants to boast of his own weakness. This expresses his intention well; paradoxically, the grace of God is visible on this earth only in weakness, even if communion with Christ in the present is real. But it is outside human control, because it is given by God. However, we should note that Paul will say later (v.10) that in weakness he is strong, i.e. he is even stronger than his opponents, who similarly boast of their visions. In other words, in this world weakness has paradoxically more power than strength.

[6a] This takes up v.5a and emphasizes Paul's right to boast of his journey to heaven. Here the theme of being a fool refers back to II Cor.11.1,16,19, and II Cor.12.11 shows that Paul regards II Cor.12.1–10 as a matter of being compelled to speak as a fool, i.e. to commend himself. However, this defence against the attacks of others should really have been the task of the Corinthians. To understand 'boast' better, we need to supplement it with either 'about the visions' or 'about something other than weakness'.

[6b] The phrase 'than he sees in me or hears from me' is enigmatic, and explanations vary accordingly. What is probably meant is that the Corinthians' image of Paul is not to be based on such experiences of glory as Paul had, which cannot be verified, but on *their* experiences of him.

Paul claims that he can keep up with the 'arch-apostles' when it comes to visions (v.6a), but at the same time he emphasizes the other characteristics of an apostle: this is, first, a life in weakness and persecution, which is made effective only by God's grace. There are external indications of this life, like suffering and sickness. Furthermore, it is a characteristic of the apostle to proclaim the gospel.

[7] What 'and the abundance of revelations' refers to is unclear. The words can be related either to v.6 or to v.7. In the first instance the clause would explain why someone could deem the apostle higher than he or she otherwise would do on the basis of their own perceptions, namely because of the abundance, i.e. the high value, of his visions. If the phrase is to be referred to v.7, then Paul is anticipating the key word 'revelations', which becomes the main theme of the whole of the next section and links vv.7b–9a with what has gone before (vv.6–7a) by 'therefore'. However, in terms of content there is no difference between the two possibilities.

The word 'elate' provides a framework for the statement in v.7. This verse contains the interesting biographical detail that Paul was afflicted by an angel of Satan so that he did not exalt himself above others. Here we have a mythical description of an illness of Paul's. The expression 'angel of Satan' presupposes that the angels which serve Satan are subject to him (cf. Matt.25.41; Rev.12.9 etc.), and that Satan, his angels and evil demons cause illnesses. *So for Paul vision and illness belong inseparably together.*[112] The extraordinary revelations are accompanied by an illness, so that Paul does not 'exalt' himself above others. The idea of self-exultation or self-exaltation is a Jewish notion (cf. Ezek.21.31; James 5.10; I Peter 5.6). Those who exalt themselves will be punished or brought down. Thus Paul is evidently explaining to himself the juxtaposition of revelation and sickness in his own person.

[8–9] These verses explain that the power which is expressed in these revelations will become even more powerful through the combination of vision and sickness. Verse 8 contains assured evidence for prayer to Jesus which is otherwise only rarely attested in the letters of Paul (cf. I Cor.1.2, 'Call on the name of the Lord'; I Thess.3.11f.). The threefold prayer reflects a current Jewish custom (cf. Dan.6.11) and expresses the urgency of the prayer (cf. Matt.7.7). Verse 9a formulates the answer to Paul's prayer in the form of a 'healing oracle',[113] even if a healing is refused.

Probably the event described from v.8 on is similarly an ecstatic experience (audition, v.9a) which is still part of the same event as vv.2–4, or which for Paul has fused to become one event in the remembrance. At least Paul understands both events, the 'ascension' and the interpretation of his weakness by the heavenly Christ, as related (in content).

[9b] In this clause Paul produces another summary, now as a remark of his own. In so doing he accepts the word of the Lord as a meaningful interpretation of his situation.

[10a] This gives a resumé of the events reported in II Cor.11.24ff., and v.10b ('for when I am weak, then I am strong') makes a weighty conclusion.

The appearance of Christ to Paul: A vision!

One important result of the previous section is the conclusion that in II Cor.12 Paul depicts a journey to heaven or a rapture which is combined with a vision in which he saw paradise and the heavenly Lord. This vision was combined with an illness. Paul sees the sickness as reinforcing the vision, so that it becomes an expression of the overwhelming power of Christ.

On this basis we can now define the relationship of the call vision (= the Damascus event) to the vision in II Cor.12. There is no disputing the fact that in the visions of Jesus after the Damascus event Paul experienced his encounter with the 'Exalted One' just as really as on the first occasion. Only a little religious sensitivity leads to the insight that the 'Damascus vision' and the 'heavenly journey' narrated in II Cor.12 belong to the same form of experience, although they are certainly not identical. In terms of the psychology of religion, 'the conversion vision and the heavenly journey are two different events: in the first instance Christ descended and "appeared to Paul" – here Paul ascends to the Lord in heaven'.[114] However, both consist of a 'seeing' and culminate in a 'hearing' of the Lord, even if the content is different. A further reason for Paul's failure to mention the Damascus vision in II Cor.12 may be that it was already known to the Corinthians before Paul's preaching when he founded the community in Corinth, from personal oral tradition (cf. Gal.1.13–23) and from I Cor.15.8.

Here it is important that in the cases both of the vision reported in II Cor.12 and of the Damascus appearance an illness is part of the event (Acts 9.8/II Cor.12.7). According to the tradition depicted by Luke Paul became blind, whereas II Cor.12 does not allow any closer definition.[115]

What have we achieved? *We now know that Paul often had*

visions. We must assume that his conversion experience before Damascus, in which the risen Christ appeared to him, was also a vision. But the question continues to remain open who or what evoked these visions. Certainly we can now simply claim that God himself was the author of this vision and to that degree it was an original revelation. But a historical investigation of events cannot make things as easy as that for itself. For that would be to abandon scholarship and return to a speculative theological approach which needs to be avoided.

So the next question is: how do we explain the vision at Paul's calling?

Paul's conversion experience of Christ – a 'Christ complex'

Paul's pre-Christian period, which lasted until he was around thirty,[116] was stamped by a fanaticism (Phil.3.6) which expressed itself among other things in an inexorable persecution of Christians (Gal.1.23). The reasons for this lay first in the proclamation of the crucified Messiah, secondly in the Christian criticism of temple worship and thirdly – closely connected with this – in the disregard of the Jewish law in social dealings with Gentiles (Gentile Christians). But whereas Saul massively persecuted the Christians, other Jews like 'Gamaliel' counselled waiting (cf. Acts 5.38f.). Thus it is clear that the preaching of the early Christians did not automatically provoke persecution. Rather, the persecution came from a particular Jewish group to which Saul also belonged.

The sources tell us little about the change in Paul from persecuting Christians to proclaiming Christ (from 'Saul' to 'Paul'). Reference should be made to the passages analysed above (102–25) and to Gal.1.23 ('He who once persecuted us is now preaching the faith he once tried to destroy') as oral tradition in the churches of Syria about the sudden change in the persecutor of Christians.

The use of Romans 7 to understand the shift in Paul's life story, which was once so popular, has now been abandoned almost everywhere. In this chapter Paul describes the history of his ego and the rift in it before he turned to Christ.

> 7.7. Is the law sin? By no means! Yet, if it had not been for the law, I should not have known sin. I should not have known what it is to covet if the law had not said, 'You shall not covet' (Exod.20.17).

8. But sin, finding opportunity in the commandment, wrought in me all kinds of covetousness. Apart from the law, sin lies dead.

9. I was once alive apart from the law, but when the commandment came, sin revived and I died;

10. the very commandment which promised life proved to be death to me.

. . .

14. We know that the law is spiritual; but I am carnal, sold under sin.

. . .

18. For I know that nothing good dwells within me, that is, in my flesh. I can will what is right, but I cannot do it.

19. For I do not do the good I want, but the evil I do not want is what I do.

. . .

23. But I see in my members another law at war with the law of my mind and making me captive to the law of sin which dwells in my members.

24. Wretched man that I am! Who will deliver me from this body of death?

25. Thanks be to God through Jesus Christ, our Lord!

Since the classic work of Werner Georg Kümmel in 1929[117] three objections have been made to a biographical understanding of the first person:

1. Here as e.g. in the Psalms, the first person is a stylistic form;

2. Romans 7 is to be understood in its context: in the form of a retrospect it gives a theological, not a historical, description of the pre-Christian self;

3. In other passages like Phil.3.6 (I was 'blameless as to righteousness under the law') Paul does not give any indication of the split in his pre-Christian life.

In criticism of the first two points it has to be said that they do not rule out a biographical understanding. The reference to the theological form of this retrospect does not necessarily rule out the historical question as to how far this theological interpretation of Paul's own biography has a historical nucleus. And whether Phil.3.6 really does show a quite certain self-confidence in the pre-Christian Paul is not beyond dispute.

The question arises whether further exploration in terms of depth psychology can prompt historical reflections. This brings me to an attempt at an explanation which on the one hand may increase our knowledge about the conversion of Paul and on the other help us to grasp its significance. As a theoretical model, one can use a psychodynamic approach which understands religion as a grappling with the unconscious.[118] This model of an interpretation in terms of depth psychology should contribute towards understanding Paul in terms of the world in which he lived.

As I have pointed out above, the source text indicates that the pre-Christian Paul was a committed, indeed fanatical, persecutor of Christians. This striking behaviour suggests that the basic elements of the preaching of Christians had a very strong effect on him. His encounter with Christians and their preaching and practice took place not only at the level of understanding but at the same time at a conscious and unconscious emotional level – a phenomenon which applies to all experiences. Underlying Paul's vehemently aggressive attitude to Christians was presumably an inner personal inability which depth psychology has established to be a frequent cause of aggressive behaviour. In general this inability is expressed in the attraction of someone by something that goes against his principles. Such a person may not or will not therefore yield to it. So he attempts to suppress this feeling by force, so that it does not gain the upper hand and bring down all his principles. But the more he does this, the more he comes to hate others who can openly express the same feeling, since they can do what he is laboriously seeking to combat. This leads to hatred of his own situation, i.e. in the end of himself, in the hatred of these other people. He projects – to use the technical term – his hatred on others. He becomes a fanatic.

Fanatics must often suppress the doubt in their own views and practices if they are not to destroy themselves. If this is true of Paul,[119] his religious zeal was a kind of thermometer of his inner impotence, which finally released itself in a vision of Christ. Perhaps we can follow Jung in saying that Saul was unconsciously a Christian even before his conversion.[120] In that case he would have had a Christ complex of which he was unconscious. This may have formally been brought to the boil by the Christians whom he persecuted. He wanted to find relief by engaging in an external combat. That became his 'doom'. Saul became Paul.

What may we suppose to have been the content of this Christ complex? First, it may have been connected with the law. Romans 7 formulates in retrospect the unconscious conflict which Paul endured before his conversion. Secondly, the conflict could have been sparked off by the proclamation of the crucified Christ (a crucified figure could not be the Messiah), thirdly by the universalist tendencies of the preaching of Christians whom he persecuted, and fourthly by Jesus' preaching of love, which was also disseminated by the Christians.

What Paul found unimaginable was that in the human being Jesus what he himself had always longed for unconsciously had become reality. Paul's idea of Christ, first brought to the point of breakthrough by the preaching of those whom he persecuted, has a parallel in the activity of Jesus. At the same time the historical cross of Jesus gave Paul's image of Christ a previously unknown dimension. Paul may have experienced and understood his change from persecutor to preacher as an experience of life, as an experience of eternity, as liberation from the law and from sin. For all these themes are discussed in Rom.7 (vv.10,23f.; cf. I Cor.15.56). Here it is almost impossible to decide whether Paul could have said that in this form immediately after Damascus. Certainly he reflected on his vision, but the problem behind Romans 7 is too 'loaded with experience' for it to have been conceived of and developed in an exclusively theoretical way. Now if what Paul overcame here was a real conflict, then historically it has to be put close to the Damascus event.

Conclusions from the analyses of the appearances of Christ

The critical investigation of the various resurrection appearances produced a surprising result: they can all be explained as visions. Here those of Peter and Paul are to be termed the original visions, because they took place without *external* catalysts.

Peter received the first vision, which is to be interpreted psychologically as failed mourning and the overcoming of a severe guilt complex. He had 'sinned' against Jesus by denying him. But under the impact of Jesus' preaching and death, through an appearance of the 'Risen Christ', Peter once again referred to himself God's word of forgiveness which was already present in the activity of Jesus, this time in its profound clarity.

This first vision became the initial spark which prompted the further series of visions mentioned by Paul in I Cor.15. The subsequent appearance of Christ can be explained as mass psychoses (or mass hysteria). This phenomenon was first made possible by Peter's vision.

By contrast, Paul's appearance did not depend on Peter's vision, since here it was not a follower but an 'enemy' of Jesus or his supporters who was affected. Here Paul's biography gives strong indications that his vision of Christ is to be explained psychologically as an overcoming of a smouldering 'Christ complex' which led to severe inner (unconscious) conflicts in him and finally released itself in this vision.

Despite their independence from each other there are clear parallels between the two original visions of Peter and Paul:

1. In both, the vision of Jesus is inseparably related to the denial of Jesus or the persecution of his community.

2. In both a feeling of guilt is replaced by the certainty of grace.

3. Both figures may have put forward a doctrine of justification which was similar, indeed largely in agreement (Gal.2.15f.: 'Because *we* know that a man is not justified by works of the law but through faith in Jesus Christ'). Paul evidently agreed with Peter from the beginning that men and women are justified through faith in Christ and not through the law; indeed this conviction led both to turn to Christ in their 'Easter experience'.

However, this means that God must no longer be assumed to be the author of these visions, as is still argued frequently, but inconsistently, even by advocates of the vision hypothesis. Rather, these were psychological processes which ran their course with a degree of regularity – completely without divine intervention.

At the same time this means that the assumption of a resurrection of Jesus is completely unnecessary as a presupposition to explain these phenomena. *A consistent modern view must say farewell to the resurrection of Jesus as a historical event.*

4

Consequences of the Results
of the Investigation

The origin and essence of the earliest Christian belief in the resurrection

According to the evidence of all the New Testament Gospels, the Roman prefect Pontius Pilate had Jesus crucified on a Friday (around the year 30). His disciples who had come with him from Galilee to Jerusalem for the Passover abandoned him and fled before or at his arrest. The last to flee after some hesitation was Simon Peter, one of the Twelve, who had a pre-eminent position among the disciples. By contrast, women followers of Jesus, who had also travelled with their Master, stayed with him longer. They included Mary from the Galilean fishing village of Magdala, whom Jesus had healed of a serious illness (Luke 8.2).

The motives for the execution of Jesus by the Roman Pilate are clear. He saw him as a political troublemaker, who had to be put out of action. Evidently Jesus was falsely accused of being a political agitator by elements of the Jerusalem priesthood who were hostile to him, as he appeared to be an eschatological Messiah. To what degree a disciple (Judas) was also involved is uncertain.

The trial, execution and death of Jesus took place on the same day. This was followed by the sabbath, which in that year coincided with the first day of the feast of Passover.[121] This posed a problem for the Jews about what do with the body of Jesus, since according to Jewish custom it was not permissible to leave a corpse on the cross overnight (Deut.21.23), and moreover on a sabbath which in addition was part of the Passover. At all events, the Jews were given permission by Pilate to take the body of Jesus down from the cross. Either the Jews entrusted Joseph of Arimathea with putting the body of Jesus in a tomb or Jews unknown to us 'buried' the corpse in a place which can no longer be identified. That settled matters for the relevant Jewish authorities and Pilate, in whose view Jesus of Nazareth was only one of many Jewish messianic pretenders.

No one knows what Jesus felt like in his last hours. The words attributed to him during the trial and on the cross are certainly later creations. Nor can it be said, for example, whether he really collapsed inwardly, as is often claimed.

So Good Friday ended in a catastrophe and thus the torch lit by Jesus was evidently snuffed out by an icy blast. However, not long after the death of their Master on the cross and their return to Galilee a new spring unexpectedly dawned for the disciples. We do not know precisely when this happened. That it was on the third day, i.e. on the Sunday after the sabbath, can be ruled out above all because the breakthrough took place in Galilee and the disciples cannot have got back there in one or two days (and moreover during the sabbath). But not long after the Friday on which Jesus died, Peter experienced the living Jesus in a vision and this event led to an incomparable chain reaction. If Peter had seen and heard Jesus, this content of the appearance of Christ was handed on to others. The news spread like lightning that God had transported or exalted Jesus to himself. In other words, God had taken the side of Jesus, something which had not been expected after Jesus' death on the cross. From this the conclusion was drawn that God was speaking to men and women in the crucified Jesus. Soon he would return as judge of the world. That created a new situation, and the Jesus movement embarked on a tremendous new beginning. Now the followers of Jesus could go to Jerusalem again and there take up the work which their Master had left incomplete; they called the people and its elite leadership to repent. Perhaps the present was understood as the last respite that God had given.

Since Peter had experienced the forgiveness of sins in particular in the breakthrough of a guilt feeling, first it was certain that the experience of the crucified Jesus was directly connected with the forgiveness of sins. So the experience of the forgiveness of sins became an essential part of the earliest Christian Easter faith. Secondly, the Easter faith developed as an experience of the overcoming of death, i.e. as experience of the life which from then on influenced the community as spirit. This life streamed into a vision in the present. Real eternal life was experienced there and then; the future became present. To this degree, thirdly, the earliest Christian

Easter faith is also a belief in eternity and as such an 'eschatological' faith. Time and eternity have become one in such a way as to open up a perspective on eternity. Eternal life has become human life.

The first vision to Peter proved formally infectious; it was followed by others. The group of twelve which was founded by Jesus during his lifetime was carried along by Peter and also 'saw' Jesus. And probably at the Feast of Weeks which followed the Passover at which Jesus died, the appearance to more than 500 took place.

Women, too, were among those who saw Jesus. Indeed, when opponents on the Jewish side objected and asked where the body of Jesus was, it could immediately be reported that the women had found the tomb empty and later that Jesus had even appeared to the women at the tomb.

We cannot underestimate the explosive dynamic of the beginning with its religious enthusiasm. The physical brothers of Jesus (cf.I Cor.9.5) were also caught up in the maelstrom and went to Jerusalem. James even received an individual vision.

We should reckon that the events mentioned took hardly more than six months. Here many things went on in parallel. In addition to the experience of the resurrection, the following elements of the development can be clearly grasped historically: (a) in the breaking of the bread the assembled community immediately relived for itself fellowship with the Messiah Jesus who had been so wretchedly executed and now had been all the more powerfully endorsed; (b) the recollection of Jesus' activity and his word immediately came alive; (c) 'the eschatological-messianic word of scripture present to their minds, here above all the messianic songs of the psalter, which people had long known by heart', were now sung 'as psalms of present fulfilment, to the glory of the exalted Messiah-Son of Man'.[122]

The movement reached a new stage when Greek-speaking Jews joined it in Jerusalem. That may already have happened at the Feast of Weeks following the Passover at which Jesus died, when people from all countries were in Jerusalem and heard of Jesus. At all events, the message of Jesus spread into areas outside Jerusalem and attracted the attention of the Pharisee Saul. He went into action and suppressed the new preaching, until he was similarly overcome by Jesus in a vision before Damascus. With this event an outer point is reached in the earliest Easter faith, although Jesus also kept 'appearing' in the subsequent period. Three years after the appearance of Christ to him, Paul travelled to see Peter in Jerusalem and learned further details from him of the preaching and activity of Jesus.

This brief sketch of the events after Jesus' death naturally makes no claim to completeness. Doubtless one or other point of the historical outline of the earliest Christian belief in the resurrection needs to be corrected. 'During these momentous months of the beginning . . . many movements and discoveries alongside and with each other and sometimes confusingly "through each other" were possible. The encounters with the risen Christ formed . . . a complex knot; we can no longer neatly untangle the individual strands and put them in chronological order . . .'[123]

The resurrection faith of the earliest community and ourselves – or: can we still be Christians?

We can no longer take the statements about the resurrection of Jesus literally. However, it is certain that people at that time believed in the resurrection 'literally'. That cannot be and may not be relativized. But there is no basis for arguing that even today we must believe in the 'bloody' reality of the resurrection. That is a typical mistake which is constantly made. *If the body of Jesus was not revived, then no revival of the myths will help us.* If Jesus did not rise in that way, there are serious consequences for our religion, but they do not mean the end of it. However, from the fact that the earliest Christian religion was once bound up with belief in the revival of the body of Jesus we cannot unconditionally conclude that if we want to be proper Christians we must also believe in this revival of the corpse of Jesus today. *This was not a historical fact but a verdict of faith.* We cannot join in blindly, and we must honestly confess that.

Earliest Christian faith arose out of the interpretation *then* of an event against the background of the world-view *then*, in other words in the framework of the possibilities *then*. *Today* we interpret the same event differently, namely within the framework of *today*'s possibilities. The future may perhaps interpret the same event in yet another way. The external form of faith necessarily changes with the changed interpretation, indeed it is first made specific on the basis of the interpretation. The nucleus of faith, i.e. the event which first sparked off the different interpretations, remains unalterable here.

But the form of faith must change. For turning the doctrine of the resurrection of Jesus into a dogma runs the risk of literally carrying a piece of living religion to the grave.

So let us say quite specifically: *the tomb of Jesus was not empty, but full, and his body did not disappear, but rotted away.* Even today, or again today, many people are seeking to avoid this inevitable conclusion. But all these approaches are evasive movements where history is concerned. Here either the historical question is demoted to being a question which is marginal to theology, or theology solemnly claims to be the better form of history. But this very effort to fight against history already shows that the historical question is a decisive one which needs to be answered in our time.

With the revolution in the scientific view of the world, the statements about the resurrection of Jesus have irrevocably lost their literal meaning.[124]

In theology, the sphere of dogmatics has among other things the task of examining the contemporary value of the content of Christian faith and, if need be, of correcting it or bringing it up to date. So in this special instance of the resurrection of Jesus, too, dogmatics are required to draw the consequences of a changed situation. Here there is a great opportunity to make the Christian faith credible again. This credibility of theology, which at the same time is also the credibility of the Christian church(es), may be put in question nowadays by many factors. However, that need not be its end; it can lead to a new orientation which will result in the break-up of encrusted structures and the development of 'modern' forms.

If the traditional ideas about the resurrection of Jesus are to be regarded as finished and need to be replaced by another view, the question of course inexorably arises: are we still Christians?

Now in various ways I have already indicated that as a result of Easter faith Peter arrived at a fundamentally better understanding of the Jesus whom he knew in his lifetime. The experience of the unlimited grace of God which Peter had in personal converse with Jesus was manifested irrevocably at Easter. Moreover Easter resulted in a continuation of Jesus' practice of sharing meals. So Easter led to an experience with Jesus which further strengthened the earlier experience of Jesus during his lifetime. It was not Jesus or his message which needed the 'Easter event' but Peter and the disciples.

Finally, the historical reconstruction led to the insight that the characteristics of the Easter experience (forgiveness of sins, experience of life, experience of eternity) were already contained in the words and story of Jesus. So we have to say that before Easter, everything that was finally recognized after Easter was already present. In between, however, lay the bloody event of the cross. Through the cross – to the judgment of faith – Jesus showed himself alive to the disciples. Here no one can prove historically that Jesus deliberately took the cross upon himself; but this cannot be refuted either. Faith recognizes in the cross of Jesus the acceptance of death as an act of life.[125] It recognizes the deepest, most mysterious 'Yes' of God where the heart first of all perceives nothing but the 'no'. It sees an absolutely hidden eternity, an absolutely hidden grace and a never-failing offer of freedom where the neutral observer sees only the death of Jesus on the cross. However, faith no longer regards history in the same way as nature, but engages in constant dialogue with it and is affected by it. The necessary historical distance is preserved, and at the same time a personal attitude of hearing and seeing is involved.

Now that also means that traditional faith is not really robbed of any of its content, provided that we ask critically enough and do not regard historical research as a threat to our faith. To make the point once again: the words and story of Jesus already contained within themselves the essential characteristics of the earliest resurrection faith, so that the earliest witnesses, purged by the cross, were saying, sometimes in another language, the same thing as Jesus. *So to the question 'Can we still be Christians?' the answer is a confident 'Yes'.*

The further question, whether in addition belief in God the Father and Jesus his Son is necessary, is similarly to be answered with an emphatic affirmative, because Jesus is not an invention or a projection. The man Jesus is the objective power which represents the enduring basis of the experiences of a Christian. Through him we are 'first taken up into a true communion with God'.[126]

However, it must also be said that historical proofs are not enough. 'Jesus is a person who encounters us through historical mediation, a person who like all living persons is not bound to time in what one can perceive of their doing . . . all certainty in the personal relationship ends up in relatively doubtful material which can be disclosed only through interpretation.'[127]

So it is here, on the historical Jesus as he is presented to us in the texts and encounters us as a person through historical reconstruction, that the decision of faith is made, not on the risen Christ as we would like him to be.

However, I *believe* that this Jesus was not given over to annihilation through death. Our faith in his being with God, his exaltation and his life follow almost automatically from our communion with God – but in constant relationship to Jesus' humanity – without, however, it being possible to make statements about his present being. He is hidden from us as the Exalted One, and our access to him is only in God. We must stop at the historical Jesus, but we may believe that he is also with us as one who is alive now.

If, to sum up, the man Jesus as the ground of faith is the clue to God in our lives, and notions of faith arise from the communion with God which is opened up as a result, in conclusion the question can be asked: What are we to think about probably the most important idea of faith, the hope of resurrection? To put it concretely, what are we to think about our own future, our own death?

I believe that the unity with God experienced in faith continues beyond death. It comes to consummation in God while still in the night of death – it makes no sense to ask about events in the beyond.

Understood in this way, the Christian faith seems reduced almost to a minimum by comparison with former times, but as a result it has also become elementary. It does no harm from now on for Christians to live by the little that they really believe, not by the much that they take pains to believe. That is a great liberation, which already bears within it the germ of the new.

Notes

1. Hans Kessler, *Sucht den Lebenden nicht bei den Toten. Die Auferstehung Jesu Christi in biblischer, fundamentaltheologischer und systematischer Sicht,* ²1987, 19.
2. Jürgen Moltmann, *Theology of Hope*, 1967, 165.
3. Hans Küng, *On Being a Christian*, 1977, 381.
4. Willi Marxsen, *The Resurrection of Jesus of Nazareth*, 1970, 126f.
5. Karl Jaspers, *Der philosophische Glaube*, 1948, 61.
6. Hans Grass, *Ostergeschehen und Osterberichte,* ⁴1970, 13. His italics.
7. Hans von Campenhausen, *Der Ablauf der Osterereignisse und das leere Grab*, SAH, phil.-hist.Klasse, 1952, ⁴1977, 54.
8. Moltmann, *Theology of Hope* (n.2), 182.
9. However, the majority of theologians put the date at around 49.
10. Formulae relating to Jesus' death: Rom.5.8; 14.15; I Cor.8.11; Gal.2.21; I Thess.5.10. Formulae relating to the resurrection: Rom.4.24; 10.9; I Thess.1.10. Cf. Philipp Vielhauer, *Geschichte der urchristlichen Literatur*, 1975, 15–18.
11. Eduard Lohse, *Märtyrer und Gottesknecht*, FRLANT 64, ²1963, 113.
12. The possibility cannot be excluded that 'then', referring to further appearances which he wanted to add, was inserted by Paul instead of an original 'and'. But even then an individual appearance to Cephas remains probable.
13. We know this from fragments of a letter of the emperor Claudius (41–54), chiselled on stone, which were found in Delphi, the so-called 'Gallio inscription'.
14. Apart from the women as witnesses who appear again in v.47 and vv.44–45, and whom Matthew and Luke did not find in Mark (cf. R.Bultmann, *The History of the Synoptic Tradition*, 1968, 274).
15. Cf. Heinz-Wolfgang Kuhn, 'Die Kreuzesstrafe während der frühen Kaiserzeit. Ihre Wirklichkeit und Wertung in der Umwelt des Christentums', *ANRW* II.25.1, 1982, 648–793: 751f. (on the duration of hanging on the cross). 'Traumatic shock' or 'severe loss of blood' are often assumed to explain the brevity of Jesus' last torment (less than six hours, cf. Mark 15.25,33).

16. Cf. David Daube, *The New Testament and Rabbinic Judaism*, 1973 (= 1956), 312. The following remarks about the dishonourable burial of Jesus are made in close connection with Daube (301–24).

17. The Gospel of Peter, which was composed at a late date (middle of the second century), was never included in the New Testament.

18. Joseph 'took the Lord, washed him, wrapped him in linen and brought him into his own sepulchre, called Joseph's Garden'.

19. 'He keeps all his bones; not one of them is broken.'

20. 'I have known instances before now of men who had been crucified when this festival and holiday was at hand, being taken down and given up to their relations, in order to receive the honours of sepulture, and to enjoy such observances as are due to the dead. For it used to be considered, that even the dead ought to derive some enjoyment from the natal festival of a good emperor, and also that the sacred character of the festival ought to be regarded' (Philo, *In Flaccum* 83).

21. Cf. Joachim Jeremias, *Heiligengräber in Jesu Umwelt (Mt 23, 29; Luke 11,47). Eine Untersuchung zur Volksreligion der Zeit Jesu*, 1958, 145: 'This world of sacred tombs was a real element of the environment in which the earliest community lived. It is inconceivable that, living in this world, it could have allowed the tomb of Jesus to be forgotten. That is all the more the case since for it the one who had lain in the tomb was more than one of those just men, martyrs and prophets.' The 'rediscovery' of the tomb of Jesus in 326 has nothing to do with his real place of burial and is a pious legend.

22. Lyder Brun, *Die Auferstehung Christ in der urchristlichen Überlieferung*, 1925, 31.

23. Joachim Jeremias, *New Testament Theology I. The Proclamation of Jesus*, 1971, 300. Further references to this work are given in the text.

24. In John 12.1–18 this anonymous woman has become Mary (a sure sign of a development of the tradition).

25. Other examples of such Markan frameworks are: 1.21–28 to 6.1–6 (miracles); 6.30–44 to 8.1–9 (stories of feedings); 8.22–26 to 10.46–52 (healing of the blind); 15.40–41 to 15.47 (lists of women).

26. For the figure of this 'young man' see Gospel of Peter 9.36: two young men descend from the heaven in great splendour of light. The white garment is interpreted in Mark 9.3 as being more than earthly.

27. Andreas Linnemann, 'Die Osterbotschaft des Markus. Zur theologischen Interpretation von Mark 16, 1–8', *NTS* 26, 1980, 298–317: 305.

28. Brun, *Auferstehung* (n.22), 11.

29. The asterisk * denotes a reference to the pre-Markan tradition underlying these verses and not the literal text of Mark as it was included in the New Testament.

30. Bultmann, *History of the Synoptic Tradition* (n.14), 286.

31. Cf. Arnold Meyer, *Die Auferstehung Christi. Die Berichte über Auferstehung, Himmelfahrt und Pfingsten, ihre Enstehung, ihr geschichtlicher Hintergrund und ihre religiöse Bedeutung, Lebensfragen*, 1905, 63f.

32. Joachim Gnilka, *Das Evangelium nach Markus II*, EKK II/2, 1979, 353.

33. Here in brackets behind the relevant verses of the end of Mark are the parallel passages: vv.9f. (Luke 8.2; John 20.1,11–19); v.11 (Luke 24.11); vv.12f. (Luke 24.13–35); v.14 (Luke 24.36–43; Acts 1.4); vv.15f. (Luke 24.47); vv.17f. (Acts 16.16–18; 2.1–11; 28.3–6; 3.1–10; 9.31–35; 14.8–10; 28.8f.); v.19 (Acts 1.9; Luke 24.51); v. 20 (Acts *passim*).

34. Grass, *Ostergeschehen* (n.6), 35.

35. Here Luke smoothes over the style, as in Mark's account women had already been mentioned immediately beforehand (Mark 15.47), some of whom are identical with those in Mark 16.1. By speaking only generally of women in Luke 23.55 (and Luke 23.49), and mentioning them by name in Luke 24.10, he avoids the rough transition in Mark 16.1 (see 27f. above).

36. Cf. Joachim Jeremias, *Die Sprache des Lukasevangeliums*, KEK Sonderband, 1980, 312, on Luke 24.12.

37. Cf. Hans Conzelmann, *The Theology of St Luke*, 1960, 149–54.

38. Hans Dieter Betz, 'Ursprung und Wesen christlichen Glaubens nach der Emmäuslegende (Lk 24,13–32)', *ZTK* 66, 1969, 7–21: 12.

39. Why is he so terse at this point and why does he tell no story of the first appearance? As an attempt at an answer: the first appearance took place in Galilee and Luke had no room for it because of his Jerusalem perspective. Moreover, presumably with Luke 5.1–11 he had already transferred the first apperance to Peter into the life of Jesus (84ff.)

40. Hermann Gunkel, *Zum religionsgeschichtlichen Verständnis des Neuen Testaments*, FRLANT 1, 1903, 71. Cf. id., *Genesis*, ⁴1917, 193f.

41. Clopas is simply the Jewish pronunciation of Cleopas (cf. Theodor Zahn, *Forschungen zur Geschichte des neutestamentlichen Kanons und der altkirchlichen Literatur* VI, 1890, 343f. n.3). It is also noteworthy that John 19.25 calls one of the women at the cross 'Mary, the (wife) of Clopas'.

42. Eusebius, *Church History* III.11; IV.22.4.

43. For the parallel text John 20.19–23 see 67ff.

44. The Christian theologian Justin in the middle of the second century similarly knows this Jewish claim, in his *Dialogue with the Jew Trypho*, 108.2: 'Yet you not only have not repented, after you learned that he rose from the dead, but . . . have sent chosen and ordained men throughout all the world to proclaim that a godless and lawless heresy had sprung from one Jesus, a Galilean deceiver, whom we crucified, but his disciples stole him by night from the tomb, where he was laid when taken down from

the cross, and now deceive men by asserting that he has risen from the dead and ascended into heaven.'

45. Schneemelcher, *New Testament Apocrypha* I, 1991, 225 (Christian Maurer).

46. Schneemelcher, *New Testament Apocrypha* I, 1992, 604 (C.Detlef G.Müller).

47. Matthew uses the verb 'worship' already in 8.2; 9.18; 14.33; 15.25; 20.20; Mark, which he has before him, does not use it there. By this Matthew is indicating that the earthly Jesus already has the authority of the risen Christ.

48. Charles Harold Dodd, 'Die Erscheinungen des auferstandenen Christus' (1957), in Paul Hoffmann (ed.), *Zur neutestamentlichen Überlieferung von der Auferstehung Jesu*, WdF 522, 1988, 139–93, 297–330, here 299–305.

49. Grass, *Ostergeschehen* (n.6), 27.

50. But the combination of God, Jesus and Spirit is already prepared for in Paul; II Cor.12.31f.; II Cor.13.13; I Cor.12.4–6.

51. Matthew speaks explicitly only of eleven disciples (Matt.28.16), as do some manuscripts at I Cor.15.5. This is the result of the consideration that Judas really had to be removed from the twelve. But originally the tradition certainly reported an appearance to the 'twelve'.

52. Thorwald Lorenzen, *Der Lieblingsjünger im Johannesevangelium. Eine redaktionsgeschichtliche Studie*, SBS 55, 1971, 25f.

53. Rudolf Bultmann, *The Gospel of John*, 1971, 681.

54. Cf. Gospel of Peter 12.52; Mary Magdalene and her women friends speak at the tomb of Jesus: 'Although we could not weep and lament on that day when he was crucified, yet let us do so now at this sepulchre.'

55. Johannes Lindblom, *Gesichte und Offenbarungen. Vorstellungen von göttliche Weisungen und übernatürlichen Erscheinungen im ältesten Christentum*, 1968, 98.

56. Bultmann, *Gospel of John* (n.53), 688.

57. 'Fear of the Jews' is a general motif in the Gospel of Peter; cf. 12.52, Mary Magdalene and her friends are 'afraid that the Jews will see them'; 12.50, Mary Magdalene 'for fear of the Jews, since (they) were inflamed with wrath . . . had not done at the sepulchre of the Lord what women are wont to do to for those beloved of them who die'. The motif appears in the later parts of the resurrection or tomb tradition, where there is already a clear distinction between 'Jews' and Christians; the Jews are no longer seen as a people but in general as a community hostile to Christians. That is a further argument for the secondary or very late character of the Johannine account.

58. Bultmann, *Gospel of John* (n.53), 690.

59. Anton Dauer, *Johannes und Lukas*, 1984, 235.

60. Günther Bornkamm, Gerhard Barth and Heinz-Joachim Held, *Tradition and Interpretation in Matthew*, ²1982, 133.

61. Bultmann, *Gospel of John* (n.53), 696.

62. Nathanael or Thomas each time stand outside an event in the circle of disciples (John 1.45/20.24), are addressed (John 1.45/20.25), make an objection (John 1.46/20.25), are won over by Jesus (John 1.46/20.26f.) and express praise (John 1.49/20.28). Finally Jesus speaks once again and utters a reproach (John 1.50f./20.29. Cf. the identical sentence structure, 'Because . . . you believe/have believed').

63. Dauer, *Johannes und Lukas* (n.59), 253.

64. Ernst Haenchen, *John II*, Hermeneia, 1984, 229, mentions many further linguistic peculiarities in John 21 compared with 1–20.

65. Rudolf Schnackenburg, *The Gospel according to St John 3*, 1982, 352.

66. For what follows cf. Bultmann, *Gospel of John* (n.53), 716f.

67. Granted, it is always difficult to get anything like certain statements on this point, but the general possibility of dating back Easter stories into the life of Jesus should not be disputed. The community also thought the words of the earthly Jesus worth repeating only because at the same time they were read and understood as the words of one who was now exalted. In addition to the passages discussed, scholars have understood the following passages as original Easter narratives: Mark 6.45–52 (Jesus' walking on the lake) and the Matthaean addition Matt.14.28–31 (Peter goes to meet Jesus walking on the lake and then loses courage); Mark 9.2–8 (the transfiguration of Jesus).

68. Thus Günter Klein, 'Die Berufung des Petrus' (1967), in id., *Rekonstruktion und Interpretation*, BEvTh 50, 1969, 11–48: 28: 'If for anyone, for Peter his message coincides with his Easter experience.'

69. Emanuel Hirsch, *Osterglaube. Die Auferstehungsgeschichten und der christliche Glaube* (ed. Hans Martin Müller), 1988, 50. Bultmann, *Gospel of John* (n.53), 546 n.3, opposes this very vigorously, without giving any reasons.

70. Hirsch, *Osterglaube* (n.69), 50.

71. Bultmann, *History of the Synoptic Tradition* (n.14). Further references to this work are given in the text.

72. It is generally accepted that the Gospel of John (18.15–18,25–27) does not contain any independent tradition on the denial and can be left out of account here.

73. For the negative use of 'Nazarene' cf. Mark 1.24; 10.47; 16.6.

74. Cf. 9.32.

75. Bultmann, *History of the Synoptic Tradition* (n.14), 267. Further references to this work are given in the text.

76. Ulrich Wilckens, *Auferstehung*, 1970, 248.

77. Günter Klein, 'Die Verleugnung des Petrus' (1961), in id., *Rekonstruktion und Interpretation*, BEvTh 50, 1969, 49–90 (appendix, 90–8): 74–90.

78. M.Dibelius, *From Tradition to Gospel*, 1971, 315.

79. Yorick Spiegel, *Der Prozess des Trauerns. Analyse und Beratung*, ⁷1989. Further references to this work are given in the text (unfortunately these passages do not appear in the much abbreviated English translation, *The Grief Process*, 1978).

80. Colin Murray Parkes and Robert S.Weiss, *Recovery from Bereavement*, 1983.

81. Among earlier scholars e.g. C.Hermann Weisse, *Die evangelische Geschichte kritisch und philosophisch bearbeitet II*, 1838, 416–20, claimed this, and more recently it has been suggested e.g. by Jeremias, *Theology* (n.23), 292.

82. The Jewish Pentecost, which took place on the fiftieth day after Passover, is the Old Testament Feast of Weeks (Exod.34.22), and at the time of Jesus had also assumed the character of a harvest festival. Cf. Eduard Lohse, '*Pentekoste*', *TDNT* VI, 1968, 44–53.

83. The technical term for such a phenomenon is 'glossolalia'. What is meant is an incomprehensible jabbering of people in ecstasy which is incomprehensible to bystanders.

84. The image of 'quenching' expresses the almost archaic activity of the Spirit as fire (cf. Acts 2.3: tongues as of flame).

85. According to Acts 2.41 the event there involves around 3000 people; according to Acts 1.15 in the time after Easter around 120 brethren were assembled for the choice of Matthias to fill the circle of Twelve. Although the increase from 120 to 3000 certainly derives from Luke's tendency to illustrate the magnitude of the success of the mission, behind it there may at the same time be knowledge of a smaller but by no means tiny group of Christians in the early period, which he multiplied. Paul seems to have knowledge of the life of the 'more than 500', as the subordinate clause in I Cor.15.6 attests.

86. Gustav Le Bon, *Psychologie der Massen* (1911), with an introduction by Peter R.Hofstätter, ¹⁵1982. Further references to this work are given in the text. It should be emphasized that Le Bon is making these remarks to discredit all religion in the traditional sense. But why should the author not have some sound insights at decisive points, despite this anti-religious attitude? In what follows I am acting in accordance with Paul's motto in I Thess.5.21: 'Test everything; hold fast to what is good.'

87. Ernst Renan (*The Apostles*, 1869) describes it as follows: 'It is the characteristic of those states of mind in which ecstasy and apparitions are commonly generated, to be contagious. The history of all the great religious crises proves that these kinds of visions are catching; in an assembly of persons entertaining the same beliefs, it is enough for one member of the society to affirm that he sees or hears something supernatural, and the others will also see and hear it . . . The exaltation of individuals is transmitted to all the members; no one will be behind or confess that he is less favoured than others . . .'(70f.).

88. Renan (ibid., 77f.) depicts the process from a perspective critical of Christianity as follows: 'These first days were thus like a period of intense fever, in which the faithful, mutually inebriated, and impressing upon each other their own fancies, passed their days in constant excitement, and were lifted up with the most exalted notions. The visions multiplied without ceasing. Their evening assemblies were the usual periods for their production. When the doors were closed and all were possessed with their besetting idea, the first who fancied that he heard the sweet word *shalom* . . . gave the signal. All then listened, and very soon heard the same thing . . . In a few days a complete cycle of stories, widely differing in their details, but inspired by the same spirit of love and absolute faith, was formed and disseminated. It is the greatest of errors to suppose that legendary lore requires much time to mature; sometimes a legend is the product of a single day.'

89. The appearance 'to all the apostles' completely escapes our knowledge and must be left out of account in what follows.

90. This Gospel is supposed to have been composed in the first half of the second century.

91. The translation follows Wilhelm Schneemelcher (ed.), *New Testament Apocrypha* I, 178 (P.Vielhauer and G.Strecker).

92. Perhaps the Gospel of Thomas contains a similar situation. Saying 12 runs: 'The disciples said to Jesus: We know that you will depart from us; who is it who will be great over us? Jesus said to them: Wherever you have come, you will go to James the Just, for whose sake heaven and earth came into being.'

93. This family politics evidently also played a role outside Jerusalem: for example Bishop Polycrates of Ephesus (end of second century) was the eighth member of the same family in the see (Eusebius, *Church History* V.24.6).

94. Cf. e.g. Friedrich Pfister, 'Ekstase', *RAC* IV, 1959, 944–87; Wolfgang Speyer, *Frühes Christentum im antiken Strahlungsfeld*, WUNT 50, 1989, index s.v. 'Ekstase', with a happy use of parallels from antiquity and modern times (Nietzsche).

95. This section closely follows my work *Early Christianity according to the Traditions in Acts*, 1989, 106ff.

96. Lindblom, *Gesichte und Offenbarungen* (n.55), 48.

97. Ibid., 32.

98. Cf. especially the following texts: Job 4.12–16; Isa.6; Dan.10.4–21; Ezek.1.1–3.15; Amos 7.1–9.10.

99. Cf. only I Enoch 14; IV Ezra 3.1–9.25 (with the explanations by Hermann Gunkel in Emil Kautzsch [ed.], *Die Apokryphen und Pseudepigraphen des Alten Testaments* II, ²1962, 341f.).

100. Cf. Klaus Berger, 'Visionsberichte. Formgeschichtliche Bemerkungen über pagane hellenistische Texte und ihre frühchristliche Analogien', in id., François Vouga, Michael Wolter and Dieter Zeller, *Studien und*

Texte zur Formgeschichte, TANZ 8, 1992, 177–255 (with German translations of numerous specimen texts).

101. James M.Robinson, 'Jesus – from Easter to Valentinus (or to the Apostles' Creed)', *JBL* 101, 1982, 5–37, refers to Rev.1.13–16 as a detailed resurrection vision in the New Testament, and also to Acts 7.55f. (10).

102. Kessler, *Sucht den Lebenden nicht bei den Toten* (n.1), 221.

103. Carl Holsten, *Zum Evangelium des Paulus und Petrus*, 1868, 65. Further references to this work are given in the text.

104. Eduard Meyer, *Ursprung und Anfänge des Christentums* III, *Die Apostelgeschichte und die Anfänge des Christentums*, 1923, 238.

105. Cf. Ernst Benz, *Paulus als Visionär. Eine vergleichende Untersuchung der Visionsberichte des Paulus in der Apostelgeschichte und in den paulinischen Briefen*, AAWLM.G, 1952, no.2, 112 (36): 'The proclamation of the apostle was more strongly permeated with visionary experiences than most of his present-day exegetes are willing to accept. But this fact was known to the communities which he founded and to which he preached, and when he was speaking to them he could refer to it. His present-day readers and hearers must learn to hear the visionary tones of his message again in all their resonance and to understand his theology as the experiential theology of a visionary.'

106. *Pneuma* is Greek and means 'spirit'.

107. For the third heaven: Slavonic Enoch 18, 'And they led me round in the third heaven and placed me in the midst of paradise'; Apocalypse of Moses 37.6, God's command to the archangel Michael runs: 'Raise him (viz. Adam) to the third heaven, into paradise, and leave him there until the great fearful day which I have still to give to the world.'

108. Ernst Benz, *Die Vision. Erfahrungsformen und Bilderwelt*, 1969, 220.

109. Lindblom, *Gesichte und Offenbarungen* (n.55), 45.

110. Hans Windisch, *Der zweite Korintherbrief*, 1970 (= 1924), 377.

111. The following instances show that seeing and hearing belong inseparably together in such heavenly journeys and revelations: IV Ezra 10.55f., 'Go in and see the splendour and the glory of the building . . . Then you will hear as much as your ears can grasp and hear'; Rev.1.2, John 'bore witness to the word of God, and to the testimony of Jesus Christ, even to all he saw'.

112. Cf. Benz, *Vision* (n.108), 15–34 (on visions and illness).

113. Hans Dieter Betz, 'Eine Christus-Aretalogie bei Paulus (2Kor 12,7– 10)', *ZThK* 66, 1969, 288–305: 300.

114. Windisch, *Der zweite Korintherbrief* (n.110), 380.

115. Ulrich Heckel, 'Der Dorn im Fleisch. Die Krankheit des Paulus in 2 Kor 12,7 and Gal.4.13f.', *ZNW* 84, 1993, 65–92, has recently diagnosed the

sickness in II Cor.12.7 as severe headaches ('trigeminal neuralgia') and connected it with the suffering underlying Gal.4.13, which kept the apostle in Galatia (87–92). However, if there is a connection between II Cor.12.7 and Acts 9.8 (which Heckel does not go into at all), the hypothesis of a hysterical blindness as Paul's illness seems more likely. This hypothesis can also be connected with Gal.4.13 and Gal.6.11. According to Guido Kluxen, 'Sehstörungen des Apostel Paulus', *Deutsches Ärtzeblatt* 90, 28/29, 19 July 1933, B 1458–9, Paul was 'presumably suffering only from exhaustion as a result of heat and sun after a long journey' (B 1458).

116. In Philemon 9 Paul calls himself an 'older man', which according to the understanding of Hippocrates denotes someone up to the age of fifty-six (at any rate *presbyteros* always refers to the last stage of a person's life). The letter to Philemon was written around 55; Paul's conversion took place around 33.

117. Werner Georg Kümmel, 'Römer 7 und die Bekehrung des Paulus' (1929), = id., *Römer und das Bild des Menschen im Neuen Testament. Zwei Studien*, ThB 53, 1974, 1–160.

118. Cf. especially Gerd Theissen, *Psychological Aspects of Pauline Theology*, 1987, 1–39; Dieter Wyss, *Psychologie und Religion. Untersuchungen zur Ursprünglickeit religiösen Erlebens*, 1991, 149–58.

119. In my view the key passage is Romans 7, for the understanding of which see Theissen, *Aspects* (n.118), 181–223. Cf. also my 'Psychologische Exegese; Röm 7 als Testfall', in Friedrich Wilhelm Horn (ed.), *Bilanz und Perspektiven gegenwärtiger Auslegung des Neuen Testaments*, BZNW 75, 1994, 91–111; also, 'Zwischen Karfreitag und Ostern', in H.Verweyen, *Osterglaube ohne Auferstehung? Diskussion mit Gerd Lüdemann*, QD 155, 1995, 13–46: 33–40.

120. C.G.Jung, 'The Psychological Foundations of Belief in Spirits' (1928), in *Collected Works* 8, 1960, 301–18.

121. Cf. John 18.28; 19.14; 13.1. According to the Synoptic Gospels Friday is already the first day of Passover. But the first day of Passover is highly improbable as a date for an execution.

122. Martin Hengel, 'Psalm 110 und die Erhöhung des Auferstandenen zur Rechten Gottes', in Cilliers Breytenbach and Henning Paulsen (eds.), *Anfänge der Christologie (FS Ferdinand Hahn)*, 1991, 43–73: 69.

123. Ibid., 72.

124. Cf. C.G.Jung, 'On the Resurrection', *Collected Works* 18, *The Symbolic Life*, 1977, 692–6: 696: 'It is funny that Christians are still so pagan that they understand spiritual existence only as a body and as a physical event. I am afraid our Christian churches cannot maintain this shocking anachronism any longer.'

125. To this degree he presupposes historically that Jesus of Nazareth accepted death as life.

126. Wilhelm Herrmann, *The Communion of the Christian With God. Described on the Basis of Luther's Statements*, (⁴1903) 1972, 293.

127. Emmanuel Hirsch, *Christliche Rechenschaft I*, 1989 (= 1978), 32f.